Margaret Cornish has devoted her life to the education of young children. She was Headteacher of a Village School in Dorset for many years which she says were 'the most rewarding years of my teaching career'.

Margaret, a mother of three, later worked with students in Colleges of Education in Liverpool and Northampton, where her 'mission' was to advocate the value of *small* schools for infant and primary schoolchildren.

Now retired and living in Felixstowe in Suffolk, Margaret remains fervently convinced that *small is beautiful*.

She has also written two books on the commercial usage of canals-a subject also connected with the further development of rural areas.

PRIMARY SCHOOLS

Small is Beautiful

Margaret Cornish

PRIMARY SCHOOLS

Small is Beautiful

Vanguard Press

VANGUARD PAPERBACK

© Copyright 2002
Margaret Cornish

A CIP catalogue record for this title is
available from the British Library
ISBN 1 903489 77 6

Vanguard Press is an imprint of
Pegasus Elliot MacKenzie Publishers Ltd.
www.pegasuspublishers.com

First Published in 2002

Vanguard Press
Sheraton House Castle Park
Cambridge England

Printed & Bound in Great Britain

Dedication

Dedicated to Faith

A gifted and dedicated Teacher and a lifelong friend.

CONTENTS

Part One

A Decision

Return to teaching at the age of 40 years.
Brief reference to early life – war and disruption of career.
Marriage and children. A Village School.

First Impressions

The Building 1840 – Space and Light.
A Vision.
A Meeting with the Vicar and A Meeting with the Caretaker.

The Interview

The Managers – irrelevant questions. Gender and tradition.
An enlightened Education Office Ref. To role of Advisors and
Inspectorate. Parents as Managers.

Early Days

The Pupils – flexibility of work programmes.
Assertion of Teacher's authority over use of the Schoolroom.
Compromise – the Harvest Supper parental involvement.
School in the community.

Getting Established

Effects of my role on the family.
Growth in numbers due to closure of Private School.
A student for one year.
Appointment of second Teacher.

Changes

The curriculum – a time of change and innovation.
Social change in the structure of the village.
A new Vicar.
Controversy over the use of the Schoolroom.
Personal circumstances – I become pregnant.
Correspondences over terms of employment.

Public and Private Lives

Assessment of professional role.
The chalet at Branscombe.

Finances and Confrontation

School Fund.
Public dances in the School.
Correspondences between Headteacher, LEA and Diocesan
representative for Church Schools.

Another Decision

An Area School
One year's sabbatical
Lecturer in Philosophy of Ed. in Liverpool
Year 2000 – The Village Hall Re – visited
A Village Hall
The children transported to area School
A Concert in the Hall
A letter from Sally

Part Two

Reflections and Articles

The Interview
A Church School – the school in the community – excerpts from
("Village children" (a Soviet experience))
Experience in not enough

Letters

The Curriculum
Curriculum assessment – Enthusiasm is not enough –
Experience is not enough
Speech
The 11+ Selection examination
Comprehensive education and Parental choice
Fiona – an unique example
Competition – Co-operation
Discipline
Small Primary Schools – A teachers' forum
A letter to the Minister of Education (1963)
First Days at School – a comparative study of two children aged
5 years – one in Liverpool and one in the Village

Recurring Themes

'Small is Beautiful' – advantages for pupils and teachers
Competition – Co-operation
League Tables
Appointment and training of teachers
Teachers' own education as on-going
Opportunities for exchanges and in-depth courses
A whole-istic view of the Education system in terms of careers' structure
Role of the Advisors and the Inspectorate

Forward

This book is a personalised account of a specific situation in a time of many changes but one in which I remain convinced that Schumacher's truism that 'small is beautiful' relative to time and motion studies in the workplace has a special relevance to the Schools in which young children are initiated into the structured programmes of educational (in its widest sense) learning.

From the evidence of sporadic demonstrations when closure of the Village School is threatened most parents know this but have no corporate voice to resist the financial (often ill-informed and suspect) and pseudo-educational arguments put forward by those more concerned with facts and figures than with the health and growth of young children. In writing this account I hope to give substance to the voice of those parents who are rightly concerned about the amalgamation of their small local Schools into the institutionalised town centres. It requires little imagination to comprehend the effects that a sudden and ongoing separation for eight hours each day from the known environment of home will have upon his confidence and ability to 'learn'.

There are problems which I do not minimise but none of which cannot be overcome by informed and concerned enquiry. One of the most important of such problems is concerned with the appointment of teachers to such schools; parents as Managers, the roles of Advisors, Inspectors and LEA personnel, the School in the Community and the moral imperative for any such community are all central concerns to be examined with reference to individual situations.

My own experience of being the Headteacher of a Village

School from 1954 to 1963 convinced me that, despite early difficulties, this provided the best situation for both children and teachers in which to flourish and enjoy working and living together. Further extensive reading in psychology, sociology and philosophy has convinced me that previous belief in the value of small local Schools for young children cannot be disputed.

I spent the last ten years of my teaching career in what was then known as a Teacher Training College with a very specific aim which was to preach the gospel of small Schools for young children to the students who would teach in them; and to halt this ongoing movement to close them down, to retain them as sentimental images of a bygone age, to sell them to private developers or to transform them into much needed Village Halls.

I continue to crusade for the retention and the further provision of *Small Locality Schools* for young children.

M.C.R. 2000

A Decision

The year was 1954

I drove in my box-like Austin 7 through the narrow lanes of Dorset from my home in the north of the county to a remote village in the south-west, almost on the Devon border. There was a good cross-country route which avoided all main roads and the hedges were green with the cuckoo-green of late spring. Bluebells had replaced the primrose clumps. Larch trees and birches were etched against a sky washed clear by a recent shower. I was on my way to look at a School, a Village School where, in my fortieth year, I hoped to re-commence my career as a teacher.

'Go and take a look at Whitechurch,' the Education Officer responsible for Primary Schools had advised me after a thorough investigation into my suitability as a possible Headteacher.

I had met with approval. I was the right age, married (now that the age of the dedicated spinster was past), I dressed well (my one well-pressed suit), I did not speak with an unacceptable accent. I had been educated at a prestigious Grammar School followed by two years at a London Teacher Training College. My teaching experience had been varied enough to avoid the stereotyping of a 'typical Village School Teacher'. As I drove westwards my mind was busy with random reflections of that past career. I remembered once again my dreadful disappointment when the declaration of war against Germany prohibited the opportunity for which I had been working for the past three years. From College, I had gained a scholarship to spend a year studying French at the Sorbonne in Paris and this would give me the necessary qualification to teach French in a Secondary School. I could take the year immediately on leaving College, or in three years' time, provided that I completed a correspondence course to prove that I was still eligible. But first,

I had to teach for the three years in order to repay the interest-free loan which had enabled me to go to College.

I was a Francophile; I loved the language and spent the holidays during those three years cycling and walking around Brittany and Touraine, staying at Youth Hostels and eating the wonderful fruit and cheese and bread bought cheaply on the market stalls.

I thought back on those first three years of teaching – three years of social isolation in another Village School eastwards of Wimborne. There were around one hundred pupils aged 5 – 14 years and I taught the juniors aged 7 – 11 years. I wasn't much good and I thought wryly of the report at the end of my probationary year which state that it was uncertain how I would develop as a teacher.

My hopes and ambitions had been focused on that year in Paris. I thought of the cottage where I had lodged and the bedroom where I had spent the hours cramped at a small table reading and completing the assignments of the correspondence course. Most of the bedroom was occupied by a large four-poster bed into which I used to burrow for warmth on winter evenings. I bought my own supply of candles as my self-imposed retreat from the sitting room was viewed with disapproval. Miss B. was the Infants Teacher, had been a pupil at the School, then a Monitor and finally had achieved the status of 'uncertificated Teacher'. White-haired and upright and a staunch member of the Chapel she assumed a moral responsibility for the new young teacher, which I resented. A Miss Lemon, my predecessor, had gone off to India as a missionary and was the paragon it was hoped I would emulate. She was always referred to as 'Lemon' (at the time it was thought *modern* to use the surname – aping the public school mannerisms I suspect!) which did nothing to enhance her in my opinion!

I thought of the 'picturesque' thatched cottage reached only by a path across a field, of the well where I, being young, was expected to draw up buckets of water for our use, of chamber pots and the privy across the field at the back and I was determined that, however 'picturesque' the School House at Whitechurch might be, I would not again endure the privations of those earlier years.

My thoughts switched again to those war years when disappointment and frustration had blighted earlier aspirations. There was Oxford and the buses where I was one of the first 'clippies'. I remembered dressing up in the evenings to go to the theatre; attending public lectures in my spare time and pretending to be a student. Then I went teaching again in the East Oxford Boys' School and enjoyed it. I went to London with a friend (her husband had been killed) and enrolled at the Institut Francais in South Kensington for the Licence es Lettres and worked in all kinds and conditions of Secondary Schools.

I spent a delightful and exhausting year teaching French and English to Oxford School Certificate Standard in Balham. (Central Schools were introduced in some cities to accommodate pupils for whom there were not enough places in the Grammar Schools. These were soon to be replaced by the Secondary Modern Schools in the post war era and eventually all Secondary Schools were incorporated in the Comprehensive system.)

A second evacuation of Schools had terminated my employment in London and further discouraged any efforts to teach elsewhere. I became a canal boatwoman! [*]

Yet teaching had always been my one choice of a career and despite the erratic course it had taken there had never been any serious alternative to curb my innate conviction that to teach was the one occupation in which I aspired to succeed. Teaching 'what' and teaching 'whom' had never been very clearly defined in my mind during those early years. I had wanted to teach French and English in a Secondary School but the two years in a Training College qualified me only to teach general subjects with a specialised interest in language development with senior pupils. A University degree course was never possible at that time in terms of cost and the qualification for entry – Latin and/or matriculation; I had neither. The scholarship to the Sorbonne had been negated through the six years of war and, although it was still available to me in 1948, (I went to the British Institute in Paris to affirm that this was so), I decided instead to get married and to raise a family. I was 32 years old after all! My

---

[*] see 'Troubled Waters', published 1988

youthful ambition to be a language teacher had diminished with the years and with the obstacles to achieve my aim.

Marriage and two children had posed more problems and, for the past two years, I had been teaching a class of infants in another Village School.

My husband suffered badly from asthma and had agreed readily to my proposition that I would apply for the Headship of a similar village school so that he could give up farming to which he was ill-suited and which he had always disliked. It had been an accepted fact that he left school at the age of seventeen, when his father died, to take over the farm. There was little alternative in the 30's when unemployment was high; at least the rented farm provided a livelihood for his mother and himself. After a thyroid operation in 1953 his dwindling energy necessitated the employment of a local man, and, financially, the farm had become a liability.

I had been teaching the class of 5-7 year olds in the Village Schools three miles distant from where we lived partly to supplement our income and partly to absorb the shock of being told by the doctor that Judith, our second child, was a Mongol – a harsh word now replaced by 'Downs Syndrome'. I had *known* about cretins and Mongols from College days but my mind had closed itself against the unacceptable. A kindly woman in the village had offered to look after Judith when the possibility of supply work became available. Giles was just over 4 years old and it had been agreed that he could come to school with me. With almost the last of my savings I bought an old Austin 7 car and taught myself to drive around the back lanes of North Dorset.

My experience of teaching very young children had been negligible but there were some useful articles in Teachers' journals to provide some guidance and the very capable Head Mistress had been most helpful. Those two years had been most rewarding in every way.

The daily journey in the Austin 7 had not been so rewarding! The ineffectual braking system was always hazardous and, to negotiate a steep hill with the sharp right-hand bend at the bottom which led to the School, it was necessary to crawl down the hill in bottom gear! There was no heater and we both froze in the cold weather. Then Judith's minder announced that she and her family were leaving the village. My husband and the farm were still limping along and it became increasingly evident that provision for our future would depend upon my training and ability as a teacher. A Village School with the provision of a schoolhouse seemed to suggest a solution.

When I had first proposed my intention of applying for the Headship of a similar Village School the Head Mistress had not been encouraging. She was aware of my home situation and warned me that I would have to expect suspicion and criticism from the parents – even if I was appointed. I too, had my doubts and it was only after an intensive interview with the Education Officer that I had decided to pursue my aim. On a purely practical level to live in a Schoolhouse adjacent to my work would eliminate so many of the daily difficulties with which I was trying to cope.

I stopped the car in a muddy gateway for a drink of coffee. Opposite was a signpost leading to Rampisham, another isolated village in the hinterland of Evershot. When I had first considered the idea of being in charge of a Village School a mutual acquaintance had driven me over to Rampisham to meet the Headteacher – the only teacher. I thought of her now with appreciation and respect for the centre of interesting and exciting project work evident in the Schoolroom.

'I teach by inspiration,' she had said; and, in this present age of statistics and tests and league tables, her words are a refreshing reminder that statistical results have little to do with the creative and imaginative response to the teaching/learning situation by both teacher and pupils.

Is teaching merely an overspill of one's own enthusiasms? I wondered as I sat there thinking back on my visit. More than that, I well knew. The nuts and bolts of the skills required to accomplish the ongoing work of the children in that Schoolroom were evident at every level of achievement. Even the labels on the aquarium and objects in the museum were carefully written – some decorated.

That visit and the interview with the Education Officer had

clarified to myself the future of my own role in another such Village School. I would be a teacher of children at the onset of their education before interest and enthusiasm became blighted by an early sense of failure and by the tedious and repetitive tedium of time-filling tasks. And it would be in an environment which allowed for the irregular development of each individual child through those early formative years without the disruption of an annual change of 'class and teacher'. The added bonus would be in the limited number of pupils; mass instruction for classes of 40 was a denial of all the theories of how children learn.

Refreshed by coffee and by recollections of that School in Rampisham, I continued on my way even more convinced that, at last, I knew where my talents as a teacher could best be employed.

And so I came to Whitechurch where there was just another run-down Village School set in its walled surround of asphalt. There had been no money to spend on such buildings after the crippling expenditure of the war. Many teachers had left the classrooms for the more exciting life in the Forces – where there were *men*!

Most Village Schools, Whitechurch included, had been invaded by evacuees from towns and cities. When the war ended and most families returned home the Village Schools were left depleted and dilapidated. A crash course of one year's training for men and women in the Forces who decided to make teaching their career helped to fill the many gaps in the Schools. However, many of the newer recruits chose to live and work in the towns and advertisements for posts in the Village Schools up and down the country were constant. The choice would be mine!

First Impressions

I came into the village through the Marshwood Vale, a rural landscape still undeveloped except for the few isolated farms where I presumed some of the pupils lived. The Village was deserted as I drove slowly past the Church and a huddle of houses. The School was at the far end by a crossroads with a pub on one corner and lovely old thatched cottage across the road from the School garden.

The building was typical of those built at the beginning of the 19th century to accommodate all children aged 5 – 14 years for whom compulsory education was also to be free. *National School* was engraved starkly on a plain slab of stone set into the flint and plaster construct of the building. I knew that the term 'National School' belied its origin as a secular foundation and that it was, in fact, a Church School under the auspices and control of the Church of England which indicated that any prospective Teacher would, of necessity, have to be a practising communicant member of the Church.

The one-storey building with a bell tower at one end sat solidly in a walled-in space of asphalt which again was divided by another wall. 'Boys' and 'Girls' I thought; it would have to come down. There was no-one around and I continued my cursory survey of the site. There were two smaller buildings, one at each side and to the rear of the main building. Earth Closets, I thought grimly. The schoolhouse was incorporated into the building along its north side with wonderful views over the surrounding countryside. The encircling boundary wall extended along the front of the house and I leaned over to savour more fully the distances and the quiet of the place. It would do... it would do. I had not the slightest doubt that I would 'do' also!

The entrance door to one of the porches was open. I had written to the Vicar, who was the Chairman of the Managers, asking for permission to visit and presumed I would be expected. I knew that any form of canvassing for the post was forbidden and concluded he might be reluctant to meet a prospective candidate. However, the door was open and I went inside.

***

Space and Light

At first glance I knew that my foremost requirements for a suitable building were met. The Schoolroom ran the whole length of the building and, at a rough estimate, was 140ft long and 50ft wide. There were long, church-like windows all along the south side and high, wide windows at each end. There was no ceiling and the width was crossed by beams from which electric lights were suspended. There was plenty of space and plenty of light to accommodate the nineteen children of Primary School age I knew to be in attendance. Two large tortoise stoves, one at each end, would provide centres of heat although I guessed that much of it would be lost in the recesses of the sloping roof. Already in my mind I was fund-raising to have a ceiling installed. The only furniture consisted of a few iron-clad desks ranged along the west end of the room, two high and dilapidated cupboards and a smaller glass-fronted one containing a sad-looking collection of library books. The peeling dull-green paintwork of the doors matched that of the tongue and grooved boarding which surrounded the walls to a height of four feet from the floor. Drab and dreary; but I knew that good fresh coats of paint and emulsion could effect transformations.

A door on the inner wall at the west end led into a smaller room which once would have been the Infants' room with a gallery – seats rising in tiers – to accommodate the numbers. There was a large sink and draining boards and an electric water heater; obviously, the room was now used as a dining area. There was a ceiling in this room and it was heated by a third tortoise stove. There were the same long windows and, although the room faced north, I thought it could well be more cosy during severe winter weather than the large, south-facing room. It would also be a useful area for individual activities apart from the ongoing work in the main Schoolroom.

A good flow of water from the tap reassured me that there was good mains' supply through the Village.

***

I had good reason to be wary of the provision of such a basic necessity. My first appointment in 1934 had been in just such a Village School and the water supply for the School and Schoolhouse had been from a well. Each summer term when the well dried up children took buckets and containers (I remember a battered tin bath hung on an end wall kept especially for the purpose) to fill with water for the day's need from a nearby stream where it crossed the lane. The water had to serve all purposes; what did we drink I wonder in those days before cokes and squashes?

***

I returned to the main room and knocked at another door set centrally along the inner wall and which I guessed led into the Schoolhouse. I knocked but there was no answer and the door was locked. I stood on the dusty floor in a patch of sunlight and wondered, weighing up the advantages – space, light and heat and a Schoolhouse – and thinking of the disadvantages – those earth closets! The general air of dilapidation and the lack of books and any kind of educational equipment could be remedied. I had a vision of tables and chairs of varying sizes for flexible usage, of shelving to display apparatus, models, children's work; a record player – (the year was 1955 before the general availability of TVs, video recorders, tapes and CD's) prints for the walls, screens (to be made by ourselves) for the display of work and to create 'corners'. The roof beams would make useful supports for mobiles, diagrams and the like. I knew that my School would be a centre of activities initiated by my own interests and abilities of the children and by anyone willing and able to share in my aim to provide these nineteen children with as rich and varied a learning experience as possible. I could see areas for painting, modelling, collecting, music-making…

and books everywhere, easily available and for every level of ability; books for information, for enjoyment of language and rhyme and story, books with good illustrations... rhymes and rhythms of poetry and song filtered into my mind... I was lost in my vision of what this large dreary room could... and *would* be like when a voice from the doorway brought me back into the present.

It was the Vicar, a kindly man who was to support my enthusiasm to renew the vitality and purposefulness of the Village School.

General comments on the weather, the journey and such-like followed introductions and eased the way to more pertinent exchanges. In reply to my observation on the general depressed state of the School the Vicar told me that the present Headmistress had been ill for some time and that there had been mention of closing down the School if no suitable applicant should be available. I had the impression that I was given only the barest details of the situation. It was only later that I learned more of the effects that years of isolation as a spinster Schoolmistress in such a village had wrought upon the health and well-being of the person who, no doubt, had once been as enthusiastic as myself.

I asked about the children, surprised that I had seen none near or around the School since my arrival. I was told that most lived in outlying hamlets and farms and that those from the row of rented Council houses nearby probably had gone by bus to the town for the weekly shopping expedition. Car ownership was for the men as transport to and from work. I began to understand that the teacher in such a School, with purchase of a car impossible on her modest salary, would be extremely isolated and very dependent upon the visiting grocer and butcher for even the most basic of supplies. I would be grateful for my own primitive model bought second-hand from diminishing savings and modestly parked at some distance from the School. The forty mile trip across the downs of south-west Dorset had seemed like an expedition to the Hebrides!

I knew that the Vicar was curious about my personal situation. It was still unusual for married women to apply for such posts despite the effect that six years of war had imposed upon social patterns of family life. The war had been over for almost a decade and it was assumed by many that the old order would be re-established with the man as bread-winner and the woman as wife and housekeeper. But fashions of thought and opinions change and turn with the times and, in educational circles, it was thought that a married woman with children of her own might better understand the children of others and that her married state would be socially more acceptable!

'Your husband?' came the expected enquiry. I was prepared! My personal circumstances were not exactly 'normal' and I guessed that there would be considerable prejudice against my appointment. I could not afford to be on the defensive with the Vicar who was Chairman of the Managers. I explained that my husband was a farmer who suffered badly from asthma and, recently, had undergone an operation for a thyroid condition. He was a tenant farmer working for himself but ill-health was causing problems. The Vicar nodded sympathetically.

'Children?' he asked.

'A boy aged six and a girl aged four – a mongol,' I replied. The condition, now known as Downs' Syndrome, was little understood in those days except as a definition of idiocy. I knew that I would have to define and explain her condition if I was even to be short-listed for the post. I could have said she was backward but I had been forced to face the reality and had decided that others would need to do the same. I explained that Judith was socially quite acceptable but that her speech was limited and she would always be backward in the conventional learning attainments.

The vicar nodded again sympathetically, (What else could he do, poor man?) and added that he knew of two other children in the village who were thought to be very backward.

Would my children be pupils in the School?

I thought that the boy probably would find it easier to attend a different School but at the present I could not make such a decision. Judith definitely would attend the School when she was five. It was good for all children to learn tolerance and compassion for the difficulties of the less fortunate. It would be the parents who would resent her and it would take time to gain

27

their confidence. Children accept differences far more readily, especially if such 'differences' are explained. There would be other 'differences' and difficulties with individual children as the years passed which also would have to be accommodated. But I had not been appointed... had not even decided to apply...

The Vicar had moved away, looked out of the window and I could sense his discomfiture and uncertainty. Briefly I wondered if a male applicant would have elicited such a negative response to the 'inadequacies' of his family!

I was determined to continue the interview on a more professional level.

How did those children who lived at a distance get to the School in bad weather? I asked.

Mostly they walked or stayed at home, I was told, although parents with cars gave lifts to children on an ad hoc basis.

***

I thought of those children back in 1934 who walked 2 and 3 miles to the Village School and whom I used to thaw out with soup heated on one of the ubiquitous tortoise stoves and whose tattered boots I used to dry out while their chilblained feet warmed and itched in the home-made 'slippers' I kept ready for the bad days. How could they hope to learn when miserable with cold and hunger? But now, in 1955, there were School meals and free transport for those who lived more than 2 miles away from the school.

***

I assumed my business-like professional role as I explained my belief that the Village School could provide the best educational environment for young children and that I fully supported with Educational Officer at County Hall in his campaign to keep the Village School open and to halt the current trend to transport all children from the age of five to larger centres in the towns. But, I added, the provision of Village Schools would have to justify the expense required to modernise and equip the old, neglected buildings.

The Vicar was nodding agreement, caught up perhaps by my own enthusiasm, but then I saw a gleam of doubt shadow his eyes. What I obviously expected would cost a great deal of money and this was a Voluntary Aided Church School which meant that the Church Commissioners would be responsible for most of the cost. The LEA paid for exterior repairs. The V.A. and VC classifications were anachronistic relics from the historical past when the spurt of provision of Schools was accelerated by the zeal of two societies, one sponsored by the Church of England and the other by the Free Churches in competition with each other to provide the rudiments of literacy and numeracy for the children of the 'lower orders'.

I forbore to provoke any antagonism at this stage by reminding the Vicar that the Church Commissioners were considered to be the wealthiest estate owners in the country, although being the honest man that he was, I'm sure that he was troubled by the thought. Was it that concern or a natural delicacy which suppressed any further enquiry about my personal situation? (He told me later that my brusque business-like attitude discouraged any such interest in my personal affairs!)

Once there had been 140 pupils at this school; now there were only 19. What had happened? I asked. (I knew that the 'tops' – 11-14 year olds – had been removed from the Village Schools in 1944 but even that would not account for such a drastic drop in the numbers.) Many families had moved into the nearby town, the Vicar said; and there was also a small privately-run School in Charmouth attended by several children from the Village. Their transport was organised by parents willing to pay the low fees as they were concerned about the depressed state of the Village School and the continuing ill-health of the teacher.

I wished that I could have met the teacher but she was away on sick leave and did not return to the Village; the removal of her furniture and belongs was to be organised by a friend.

The Vicar was still reticent about the teacher and it was not possible to pursue any further enquiries about her. I moved towards one of the cupboards and opened the doors. The smell of old paper and old worm-eaten shelves could not be ignored and I suggested that a clean sweep of all the old furniture and a

29

good application of paint and emulsion would be an asset. Would there by any help available to take out the old cupboards and have a good bonfire?

'Go slowly,' advised the good Canon as if I had been appointed already. 'Many of the older generation might well resent too many changes too quickly.'

I wanted to ask him if *his* children had attended such a School and if he would consider these conditions suitable for *them*. I refrained, knowing the answer. He and his children would have been through the Public (Independent) School system; probably the alternative would never have occurred to him. There was always financial help available to make it possible for the less well-off clergy – the public image had to be maintained.

'But the cupboards and the desks,' I insisted. 'They're unhygienic – the repository of generations of germs.'

I added that there would be provision for more suitable furniture from the LEA. My confidence was based on hearsay that it was politic to ask for *everything* at the beginning of an appointment; afterwards the generosity of provision would be limited. Already I had in my mind a list which might well have daunted the cautious Vicar... and the LEA in Dorchester!

The sun shone dust-beams through the long windows (there would have to be curtains to draw in high summer when shade and a cool breeze were more conducive to work than hot, direct sunlight) and I began to enthuse about the space and the possibilities for group work and display areas.

The Vicar moved towards the door. I was presuming too much. As if to discourage my optimism he said that the School was also used for Village functions. His words sounded alarm bells for the first of the major problems with which I would have to wrestle. I looked my query.

'There's the Flower Show in June. When it rains we use the School.' I had visions of flower stalls and displays of vegetables but I did not, at the time, envisage cages of pet rabbits and guinea pigs, dog training displays, competitions involving darts and water and all the mess left behind from bales of straw, the wet and muddy feet and the 'left-overs' from refreshments.

'Miss D stacks everything in the cupboards,' the Vicar

explained. I began to understand his reluctance to have the cupboards removed.

'The local Dramatic Society,' he continued, hesitating as he sensed my lack of enthusiasm for the use of the School as a Village Hall. 'There is only one production a year.'

'What about rehearsals?' I asked. I was assured that the Reading Room was used as often as possible. My doubts subsided when I heard that there was an alternative building in the Village for the usual activities such as the Women's Institute, the Young Farmers and the Church-based occasions such as the Harvest suppers, socials and the like.

'It's very small,' the Vicar continued. 'And the Villagers prefer to use the School. We also get a small fee for its use which helps with the cost of repairs.'

It seemed to me that the 'small fee' in no way had been used to effect the very obvious need for repairs. Doubts and apprehensions surfaced again and I stated that, if I should be appointed, the School would first and foremost be used as a place of education for the children.

The Vicar too had his reservations about my possible appointment as he could foresee the problems arising from such a radical change in the old established use of the School.

He was elderly, to retire only 3 years later, and out of touch with social changes and with the upsurge of interest and study in the theories of Educational practice aligned with Piaget's researches into the psychology of learning in young children. He belonged to the old order who believed in the value of education for the lower classes only for utilitarian ends, for example, to make them more efficient servants and workers. And I too was a threat to the established order despite my invalid husband and my obvious need to work. However, he was a good man – a man of God after all – and he tried hard to accept the differences between myself and the present Headmistress. He turned back to me as another hurdle to my possible appointment occurred to him.

Was I musical? He asked, and would I be prepared to take the Church choir?

For College entrance in 1932 a basic ability to play an instrument and/or sing had been a condition for acceptance. I assured him that I played the piano and recorder and that I was well versed in Church music – nothing unusual in those days! He brightened considerably, looked at the wall clock and said that he must leave me. Mrs A. the caretaker was outside and she would answer any further questions.

He needed to escape from any further contrary factors which might still arise from the 'interview' and I was left feeling uncertain whether or not I had met with approval.

Through the window I saw him speak briefly to the caretaker. I remember Auntie Mary, as we all called her, with great affection. Although she also was coerced into a new and different regime which demanded more of her time and often must have taxed her tolerance for my less orthodox routine and organisation of the School, she never complained and was a staunch supporter even through the difficult times. She was also, with her husband, a regular member of the Church choir.

On that first meeting we discussed our families! She had one son of whom she was justly proud, a prefect at the Grammar School; he kept rabbits I learned. Also, she had three nieces all of whom were pupils in the School although one was about to leave to attend the Senior School in the autumn. She was bright, I was told, and should have passed the 11+, but the Teacher had been ill and had 'let things slide'. Her own boy had been the last from the School to have passed and that was 6 years before.

I asked about the provision of School meals and was told that they were brought out daily in containers and that they were quite good. She was also the dinner lady who served the meals and who supervised the children afterwards while the Teacher had a break. She was to be indispensable as the only other adult to share responsibility for cuts and bruises and other minor events through the days.

She told me that Miss D. was a keen gardener so we went out into the spring sunshine to lean over the wall separating the playground from the garden. It was delightful with small contrived pathways between the plots and with a ha-ha enclosed by a six foot hedge – Miss D.'s retreat, I was told. I thought it a pity that the garden did not extend right through the asphalted area for the benefit of the children.

What about the toilets? I asked. Reluctantly, she led the

way into the nearby building. Three cubicles without doors and with pitted wooden seats were not quite so revolting as I had been expecting. They were clean although the strong smell of disinfectant could not entirely combat the stronger smell from the depths of the pit below. Auntie Mary said that the pits were emptied twice a year – in the School holidays when no one was around!

And the Schoolhouse? Was there an inside toilet somewhere? We walked around to the further side and again the smell of the urinal was impossible to ignore; when the wind was in the east the smell would be directed towards the house. Beyond the urinal was another toilet with a door. Auntie Mary explained that this was the Teacher's toilet and the door was kept locked except for the odd occasion when a boy needed to do 'a big job'.

What happened when the School was used for other purposes? I asked. Auntie Mary cautiously said there had been problems.

How had they managed when she had been at School and when there had been 140 pupils? I continued. We used to go home if we lived nearby, she said; and there was a two hours break mid-day when those who lived at a distance brought sandwiches which they often ate in the homes of friends. But it had been earth closets for everyone in those days, she reminded me, with a pit at the bottom of the garden for disposal. All too well I remembered that privy across the field through the wire netting enclosure where Miss B. had kept geese and I had a flash back of that vicious old gander which used to stand guard outside the privy waiting to make a grab for my legs as I emerged until I kept a stick strategically at hand for my defence; he soon learned!

With difficulty I refrained from comment but asked about the Schoolhouse. Miss D. liked her privacy, repeated Auntie Mary evasively and she could tell me little except that there were just three rooms downstairs with three bedrooms up over. Looking at the narrow rectangle incorporated into the north side of the building, I reckoned that the rooms must be extremely small. However, there were three bedrooms and the extensive views over fields and a copse to the long mound of Lambert's

Castle on the horizon were adequate compensation for the meagre house accommodation in my opinion! There were open fires in two of the rooms, I was told and Miss D. had an electric cooker in the kitchen where a door led directly into the Schoolroom, as I had surmised on my earlier inspection. Miss D. had never invited her beyond the kitchen, said Auntie Mary; and, as curtains were drawn along the windows, no further details of the house were available.

We lingered there, leaning on the wall while she told me that the field belonged to her brother, a farmer and one of the School Managers, whose three daughters were those to whom she had referred earlier in our meeting. I thought that it would make an ideal pitch for playing rounders and that with his three girls in the School he could hardly refuse a request for its occasional use.

They wanted to use it for the Flower Show, Auntie Mary told me, but he didn't much like the idea and bought in a dozen heifers to keep there as an excuse to refuse. I could see the heifers all congregated at the further end of the field.

Finally I said that I must go and was heartened when she said she hoped I would be appointed and that we'd meet again soon. I hadn't even decided whether or not to apply but, maybe, the warmth of her words as I left tipped the balance of my decision. I knew that the goodwill of the caretaker in such a School was paramount for the harmony and well-being of all concerned.

I would depend upon her stoic dependency to light those stoves every morning through most of the year early enough to make the rooms tolerably warm by 9 am and to return before midday in order to lay up the dining tables and to receive the containers of food. There was also the cleaning, the washing up and all too often, clearing up after out own messes with paint, straw, paper etc. So often she must have been tired (sadly, she died of cancer in 1963) but she never complained.

On my return trip I stopped along the tree-lined stretch on Toller Down to reflect upon the varied impressions chasing around in my mind. Finally I decided that it was unlikely I would be considered as a suitable candidate by the Vicar whose judgement would also influence the other School Managers. The only support for my application would be from the Education Officer on the basis of my competence as a teacher and that too might be mitigated if there would be other equally well qualified candidates.

I would fill in the application form. Any final decision could only be made *if* I was selected and so, for the present, I need not concern myself.

The Interview

In February of 1955 I was called to the Village for an interview. There had been snow and the roads were icy and the residue of my enthusiasm for taking responsibility for an isolated Village School at the far end of the county had frozen along with the weather. It took all my energy each day to drive the three miles to the School where I was teaching. The thought of that cross-country journey in my unheated car and along ice treacherous roads was prohibitive.

I was about to write an apologetic refusal when my husband suffered a sever attack of asthma which scared us both. A local man had to be employed to do the milking and the routine work of the farm and I knew that it would not be possible to afford his help for any length of time. Reluctantly my husband said that I might drive his car to attend the interview. This was a great concession; Women drivers were still regarded as greatly inferior to their male partners – my husband no exception! I had never been allowed behind the wheel of the Ford Consul and his offer was too tempting to refuse! (Probably he hoped that I would...) I arranged for a friend in the Village to stay with Giles and Judith for the day while I packed sandwiches and a thermos, padded my one suit with warm woollens and set off for the forty-mile trek. I was apprehensive at first with the unfamiliar gear change position on the steering wheel but the car was so easy to drive after the vagaries of my Austin 7 that I was through Sherborne and on my way to Bridport with no difficulty at all. I smugly considered that the large black car would do much to enhance the impression I thought to make on those who would interview me! I used the main, and the not so main, roads as there was little traffic and the car was not suited to the narrow lanes of the cross-country route. I arrived in good time, warm, comfortable and confident.

The parish Church of St. Candida stood picturesquely and historically in the centre of the Village with the School at some distance, established in the class-conscious era of patronage and separation of the lower orders from the more prestigious Christians in the C. of E. hierarchy.

The six Managers were representative of the social structure of the Village with the Vicar as Chairman and Correspondent.

The Vicar's warden was a retired 'Captain'. (I never ascertained from which of the Services he was retired. He confided in me at a later date that he had voted for the other candidate as she reminded him of his old nannie!)

The Churchwarden was a local farmer and brother of Auntie Mary. He had been a pupil at the school himself and his three daughters were pupils at the present time.

A large man, sitting uncomfortably on a too small chair, was introduced as the local builder; I presumed his professional services to the Church and School made him indispensable during that period of post-war austerity.

The three ladies were:

Miss Irene W. who lived in the Church House. She was the daughter of a former Vicar and had lived in the Village for the past 30 years. (benevolent patronage)

Mrs P. a wealthy widow interested in education. Her chief function as a Manager, I was to learn, was to conduct spot checks on the register.

Mrs H. was the Parish Councillor who represented the Village on the County Council. Three of her grandchildren were to become pupils at the school later on.

The appointment of the teacher in such a school was entirely determined by such a body of people – comparable to the jury system of 'twelve good men and true' – their opinions and judgements based narrowly on their own limited experience. The only professional judgement was that of the E.O. who had taken time and trouble to give pre-interview interviews and to attend the interview in order to influence the decision.

I thought at the time – and since – that some advice and guidance to School Managers by the body of Advisors and Inspectors to help them clarify ideas on the role of the teacher in

37

such a school and to suggest the sort of questions which were relevant to their expectations would help to ensure that their choice of candidate for the post would be based upon rational appraisal rather than upon their own limited knowledge and experience.

Almost forty years later, with many such Schools opting out of local Authority control thereby placing greater emphasis on the functions and responsibilities of the Managers, it would seem that such guidance and involvement by the professional experts is to be recommended even more strongly and in most cases situations has been implemented (1996).

Many parents are now Managers and it is to be hoped that those who realise their own lack of knowledge and experience in this situation will demand advice and guidance from the body of Advisors and Inspectors and possibly from reputable Headteachers in the locality. I appreciated the fact that Mr Easton, whose judgement I respected, made the effort to attend the interview and was able to direct and influence the decision taken. That it was in my favour was important to me, not only in a personal sense, but because I knew that it had been based on a professional appraisal and assessment of my suitability for the appointment.

The interview was held in the sitting room of the Church House, home of one of the Managers, and was presided over by the Vicar. There was just one other candidate whom I had met on arrival. She was older than myself (or so it seemed to me!), unmarried (no ring) and spoke with a north country accent.

'Had she met the other Managers?' I asked.

'Only the Vicar,' she replied. The others had been in the interview room when she arrived. She had seen the school briefly but refrained from passing any comment.

Then she was called for the interview and I was left for half an hour to collect my thoughts and still to wonder whether or not I really wanted the job. Realistically, I knew that, with my family in tow, not many choices were available to me. *If* it was offered, I would accept.

My earlier confidence had evaporated but I felt slightly reassured when I saw the Education Officer sitting in a corner by the fire. I was introduced briefly to the others present. At the time I had only a vague impression of them as individuals apart from the Vicar who introduced me.

After the introductions and the preliminaries, such as re-affirming my credentials from the application form, I was asked by one of the perceptive ladies if I would not find the Village School rather quiet and irksome after my experience in London and abroad.

Would I settle?

Did I play cricket?

Did I believe in discipline? (the cane? I wondered).

Was I a communicant member of the Church?

Was I prepared to take the Church Choir?

My musicianship was limited to playing hymns and country dances; and I could sing. With incredible confidence I replied that I would.

Did I approve of the 11+ examination for entry to the local Grammar School? I remembered that the Vicar had told me that no one had passed in recent years.

My reply was conventional. The system of selection existed and I had no choice but to conform. If a child was able there was no reason for him to fail after a period of at least one year's tuition, preferably longer. (I insured myself against possible failure of the farmer's eldest daughter who was in the top group of the School!)

There was a lull in the proceedings until the E.O. quietly asked me how I proposed to organise the work with the 19 children of different ages. He was giving me the opportunity to recount ideas which we had discussed at our previous meeting. I said that I would need to know the children first to assess ability levels and weaknesses before I could devise programmes of work which would often to on an individual basis, especially in the areas of literacy and numeracy – the 3R's – I explained. Nods of approval, so I continued.

In Germany, where I had taught for two years just after the war, I had used the Dalton plan for working with a very mixed group of junior school children. There were French, Belgians, Czechs and Yugo-Slavs whose parents (from the embassies) were chiefly concerned for their children to learn the English language. There was also a small group of British children whose parents naturally were anxious for them to be coached for the 11+ examination when and if they should return to Britain. I had devised weekly assignments of work in what I considered to be the basic subject areas for each child, grouping where possible. There had to be ongoing programmes of work which enabled me to engage in oral work with individuals and groups. The written assignments were checked each week and careful records kept of progress and problems. It entailed a great deal of work. Group activities such as Drama, Dance, Music, and some local History and Geography were taken informally and often in French or German as the need arose. (I had taken a course in German at the Regent St. Poly. prior to embarking for Germany.)

As briefly as possible, I explained that I would use a similar method in the village school.

There was some head nodding but, although I had tried to keep the interview on a strictly professional level, the doubts and suspicions about my personal circumstances took precedence over my professional ability in the minds of those present. A previous Master had been married but there had been no children and all subsequent women Head teachers had been spinsters.

'What about your husband?' asked the farmer.

(What about him? I thought but restrained my irritation.) I explained that he suffered from chronic asthma and that he would probably find work when he was stronger.

There was some hesitation and uncertainty in asking about my handicapped daughter. They were too ignorant of the condition, and too embarrassed to ask.

I had discussed the matter fully with Mr Easton and said that I proposed to accommodate Judith in the school. Children need to learn about and to tolerate differences and inadequacies in others. The Vicar had told me that there were two other 'backward' children in the village whose parents were apprehensive about the new appointment, concerned that their children might be sent away to Special School and so be further stigmatised. He also told me that there was a boy of nine who had suffered from a TB hip and who still wore a caliper; of another boy who stammered badly and of a girl whose eyesight was impaired by an early attach of measles. In the first village school where I had taught there were many handicaps to learning caused by malnutrition, by long spells of absenteeism and by limited intelligence (often the result of in-breeding). Obviously I was motivated by concern for Judith and by my need to be employed but it seemed to me that most children have some degree of handicap – at least some of the time – be it mental, physical and/or emotional which can affect motivation and ability to learn.

Finally:-

'Your daughter?' asked Miss W.

The Vicar replied on my behalf, mentioned the two 'backward' children by name and said that I had fully agreed to keep them in the village school and that there was little difference between them and my daughter. I sensed a withdrawal of approval. An ailing husband and an emphasis of interest in backward, even handicapped, children boded ill for the tuition of the ordinary, even bright children, several of whom would be related to some of the Mangers.

I would not be appointed. The vote would be in the favour of the unmarried teacher with no attachments and who fitted in more closely with the old familiar stereotype of the spinster teacher. The fact that the present teacher had been adversely criticised and ostracised until forced to take premature retirement was in the past, conveniently irrelevant to the present appointment. I could see a repetition of the same pattern. So could the Education Officer who quietly but incisively re-affirmed my professional qualifications and experience. Also I could play the piano and recorder and the other applicant had no musical qualifications.

The interview was at an end and I retreated to join the other applicant who commented on the length of time I had been absent which, in her opinion, indicated that I was the one who would be chosen.

We waited for a further lengthy period, sustained by cups of tea brought to us by a middle-aged lady who informed us that she too lived in the Church House and that she was the widow of a former Vicar. She said how important it was for the village to keep the school open and we both agreed, each no doubt wondering whose responsibility it would be to ensure that it

41

would be so.

I was narrowly appointed, the casting vote in my favour being put by the Vicar as Chairman of the Managers.

Should there have been a more unanimous decision to ensure support for the probable changes I had outlined? Significantly, I was told afterwards that the three ladies had been for me and the three men against! I knew the men would sympathise with my husband and was aware that my success as a teacher of their children would have to more than compensate for my questionable family background. I was re-called to be told the decision and asked if I would accept. The question was a formality but the smell of those earth closets made me hesitate.

'Is there anything you wish to ask?' queried the Vicar.

Those earth closets.

The pits were emptied twice a year, I was told.

I was not reassured.

Would funds be available install flush toilets and a septic tank drainage? I asked.

I also added, for good measure, that with a husband and two children, a bathroom in the school house would be essential.

Miss W. and Miss D. and the Captain were with me, nodding agreement; the Vicar looked embarrassed; the other three sceptical and silent. (What had been good enough for them...)

Again the Education Officer came to the rescue. Half the cost would be met by the LEA and he was certain that the rest would be met from funds allocated to the upkeep of Church Schools by the Church Commissioners.

So it was agreed. A septic tank to serve both the school and the house would be built in the adjoining field and a bathroom would be added over a porch erected to protect the 'front' door of the house from the north winds.

Until the work was completed my family and I were to be housed in a cottage belonging to one of the farmers; it was to be as unsanitary as conditions in the existing school house!

However, I accepted the appointment and agreed to take up my duties in the Autumn term. I thanked the Managers and added the platitudes expected from the successful candidate. I left with the Education Officer who said that he wished me well and that 'it was now up to me'. No doubt he had more understanding of the difficulties ahead than it was possible for me to imagine!

I drove slowly, not seeing the hedgerows but with eyes turned inward upon reflections of the day's events.

At the top of Toller down I stopped the car once again to walk along the ridge overlooking Beaminster and the spread of farmland and copses, above and away from the recent close encounters with a disparate group of people whose goodwill and support I would need to enlist if the village school was to be resurrected from its ashes of neglect and dis-esteem.

It was good to walk, however briefly, away from the interrogations, opinions, controversies, commitments – personal as well as professional. I would be submerged soon enough on my return home by all the practical and emotional difficulties that such a change of direction would incur for my husband as well as for myself.

Meanwhile, the sting of an early evening breeze sharpened my walk along the old trackway and walking, as always, cleared my head of all the noisy confusion of thoughts. The decision was taken. The rest would follow. I would enjoy my brief respite from the weighted anchor of future responsibilities.

Early Days

During the August after my appointment I was able to make one more visit to the village and to stay there for a few days in order to concentrate thoughts and to plan for the term ahead.

I stayed in the Church house with Miss W. one of the Managers. She was to be a great ally in the coming months and her death, two years later, was a sad loss to me. It was so necessary to have someone knowledgeable, discreet and sympathetic with whom to discuss the children and their families.

She too advised me to 'go slowly'. People find change disturbing, she said, and a threat to their own established beliefs and practices acquired and held by custom rather than by rational appraisal. It would always take a great deal of explanation and time to allay suspicion and criticism. Unfortunately, there was never enough time and energy to respond adequately to all the misgivings my changes aroused. The demands of my own family put limits upon meetings and discussions with the parents which are so essential in such a situation.

I spent most of the time during those few days sitting in one of the bedrooms of the schoolhouse using the wide window sill as a table and with a chair borrowed from Miss W. (The only chair in the school room was the teacher's chair, heavy and immovable.) It was here that I could ensure privacy from distractions of workmen and casual callers in order to compile lists of essential supplies from the few educational catalogues I had found lying in a heap where they had been delivered. I knew that orders would be pruned severely by the accountancy department of the LEA so I made them generous within the bounds of acceptability. Books, assortments of paper, pencils (biros were just about to become available) paints and apparatus for weighing and measuring and further apparatus for the younger ones, balls and hoops and ropes, – but, above all, *books*. The lists eventually were finalised and posted hopefully to Dorchester where I knew they would be scrutinised by the Education Officer who had backed my appointment.

I also committed to paper outlines of work programmes I would initiate with the pupils as soon as possible. There were five girls and three boys in the upper range of 9-11 years, three girls and two boys aged 5-7 years and four girls and two boys aged 7-9 years. 12 girls and 7 boys. 19 children. What joy after wrestling with those classes of 30 and 40 pupils on the yearly conveyor-belt system.

All good and effective teaching/learning situations are based on the one-to-one relationship between the teacher and the pupil whatever the age and whatever the ability/interest range of the pupil. The teacher leads, guides, encourages, corrects and disciplines the growth and development of each individual intellectually, socially and morally within the framework of their shared scholastic experience. If that sounds weighted and onerous, it is meant to be. There is no responsibility of greater value to the human race than the proper care of its young. Luckily, we don't take it all too seriously for most of the time but neither parent nor teacher can escape from the implications of this precept.

I look at the yellowed photograph of those first pupils and myself taken in 1956 by Kents of Bridport and printed under the caption, 'Happiest Days of their Lives'. (Judith on extreme left of front row.) I like to think this was so for most of them for most of the time. For myself, those ten years were, without a doubt, among the happiest and most rewarding of my teaching career.

First Term

I look again at that early photo of myself and the pupils for whom I was responsible and remember that first morning. Another steep hill from the rented cottage presented no difficulties.

It was only a mile from the school after all and there was the consoling thought that I could walk on the occasion when the engine would not start (cranking by handle!). It was 8.30am and there were children and a few mothers waiting in the playground, curious to see the new teacher – an event as my predecessor had been there for the past twenty years. I drove carefully and with a show of expertise manoeuvred the car through the school gates. A woman driver was still a rarity and I needed to demonstrate competence!

I asked the mothers to come into the schoolroom, surprised that they had not already done so as rain was threatening. Mrs A. (Auntie Mary) had the two tortoise stoves glowing and the room was pleasantly warm despite the escape of heat over and above the rafters! The new tables and desks on which some of the equipment ordered for the younger ones was displayed and inspected by the children and admired by their mothers. The old cupboards were still there and I explained briefly that I hoped to dispense with them and that I hoped for help to put up shelving along the walls so that books and apparatus would be more easily accessible.

Then it was 9am and I was left alone with the children although I guessed that the mothers would not have gone far. Chairs and mats were brought for seating as I would need to explain how the day was to be organised after our first assembly together. Kay chose a hymn which I was told they all knew. Those who did not know the words could hum, I suggested. Most of them started to hum! I stopped it at the end of the first

verse, said a brief prayer that God would bless this school and…
(all who sailed in her?). This was followed by the ritual of
marking the register and then we were launched into our first
day's work together. I divided the nineteen children into three
groups according to age. It would take a day or two to get to
know them, to assess ability levels and to devise suitable work
programmes at individual and group levels. Meanwhile I
encouraged the older ones to explore and arrange books and
materials I had ordered and to write introductions of themselves
while I spent time with the younger ones to get them involved
with using some of the apparatus on display. It was all very
informal and the day passed quickly enough. Surprising how
much one could learn about those nineteen children in just one
day and without the need for any tests!

As the days passed a flexible routine of work became
established and I was fully occupied with all the individual
coaching necessary in language and numeracy development. My
own love of literature, the countryside, music and crafts
provided some of the struts upon which the developing learning
programmes were based. At all times the creative spark, which I
know is inherent in all children, was to be encouraged even at
the occasional cost of insistence upon dotted i's and crossed t's.
It is better to enjoy singing, writing, thatching, painting or
whatever, than to be deterred by constant referral to mistakes.
The spark is so easily discouraged, diminished, destroyed; its
loss difficult to restore and often irreparable. Inevitably, there
comes a time when the teacher adjusts the balance between the
need to create and the need for accuracy and improvement until
– eventually (and not inevitably!) – the student begins to impose
his own discipline upon the creative impetus. Even in the
Primary School, children begin to criticise and evaluate their
work if helped to do so by the discerning teacher. But to insist
upon the formalities of procedures before the enjoyments and
excitement of the project has been experienced is like putting the
proverbial cart before the horse – and no one gets anywhere!

It would seem that all was set fair for my efforts to establish
the village school as a reputable centre of learning and
enlightenment. No so. During that first term I began to
understand reasons why competent teachers preferred to work in

the municipal schools and why – at that time – so many of the village schools were almost derelict with the buildings in disrepair and many of the teachers isolated and demoralised. Almost all of these teachers in the one/two teacher rural schools were spinster women. When the 'tops' (11-14 year olds) were removed from the all-through village schools to be centralised in senior schools (later to be classified as Secondary Modern) most of the men head teachers chose to be transferred to these senior schools as professional prestige was linked to the age of the children being taught. (With the current political/financial proposition that unqualified persons be employed to 'teach' the younger children it would seem that such quixotic and outmoded notions are to be revived despite all the years of research into the psychology of how children learn which demonstrate explicitly that those early years in a child's education – for good or ill – are of fundamental importance to his future development and achievement.)

Almost the only Headships available to women in State Education pre-1940 were those of Infants' School (5-7 year olds).

Now there was move to appoint women as Heads of the decapitated village schools – it was cheaper after all! (Equal pay for equal work had yet to be achieved); but in rural England, male dominance was still the accepted social order and to replace the 'Master' – as the Head was often called – with a spinster teacher (married women were not employed until 1940) was not admissible to the majority of the villagers. Any authority she could exert outside the actual boundaries of the school depended heavily upon the co-operation and approval of the Vicar/Rector and any other person of influence who lived in the immediate area. Socially she was isolated. The Vicar, Doctor etc. had been educated in the Independent fee-paying schools, had been to University whereas the teacher's education had been in a Grammar school followed by two years in a Teacher Training College. The class system was firmly established in the villages and was strictly adhered to by all. The single woman teacher had no place and was seldom accorded acceptance and affection as recorded by 'Miss Read' in her books about the village of Thrush Green. Too often she was pilloried by those who wished to 'cock a snook' at those in authority – an Aunt

Sally of the fairground! Small wonder that many such Headteachers chose to vacate the schoolhouses to live elsewhere than in the villages where they taught and, with the growing availability of cars, this became possible.

My predecessor had not 'escaped' and had sought refuge in her garden. For practical reasons the provision of the adjoining schoolhouse at a nominal rent was necessary for me with a family. I also believed – and still do – that the school should be a focal place in the village and that the teacher(s) should integrate as far as possible – and was desirable – in the life and lives of the community. (Only later was I forced to find an 'escape' for myself and the family.)

But I was still at the mercy of old traditions and practices. Even though I was a married woman with a family (and my husband was never an authoritative person) I was still only a woman. The work to provide drainage and sanitation for both the school and the schoolhouse was undertaken by a local builder and, for various reasons, had been delayed continually. During that first term a couple of workmen sporadically dug trenches and laid pipes. Most of the time they were unsupervised and, what better opportunity to get even with old grudges against authority, than to pester the new teacher. They did everything to distract the older pupils (still uncertain in their response to my expectations) by tapping at windows, playing football in the playground and using an electric drill when it was thought to cause the most distraction. I asked, reasoned, threatened and eventually told the Vicar that the school would have to be closed until further disruption was removed. It was impossible to work under such conditions, and the builder should accept responsibility for his workmen. The Vicar was a kindly man, not too well and little was done until I wrote to the Education Officer in Dorchester. (There was no phone in the school until I was able to insist on one being installed in case of injury or emergency!)

Mr Easton, the Officer who had supported my appointment, continued to be a great ally. He had been a teacher himself and was keen to promote the standards of teaching in the rural schools. He came to visit, assessed the situation and a meeting with the Managers and the builder was called. Although the work to construct a septic tank, to build a bathroom and to install water closets was protracted, further disruption by the workmen was minimal. The work was completed by the following Easter and we were able to move into the schoolhouse during the ensuing summer holiday.

Mr Easton reinforced advice already given by the Vicar and Miss W. that I should 'go slowly' and not to antagonise those on whose services I might need to depend. But the changes were to be more than structural and, although I was able to tolerate delays in the building programme my work with the children in this time of transition from formal class instruction to more informal individual and group teaching could not be delayed. During that first year there was suspicion – even antagonism – as well as curiosity from many parents who had been pupils at the school under a more formal and rigid routine. I knew that results and explanations would in time, diffuse their criticisms. Mr Easton's visit and further discussions with him about the value of village schools to the community did much to encourage me in those early days.

It was perhaps fortunate that my husband and the children had remained in the farmhouse during that first term so that I was able to concentrate on the schoolwork during the week. The trek back across the county in the old Austin 7 at the weekends was often hazardous in bad weather and the two days at home were more than fully occupied in preparations for the week ahead. Mrs A. and my husband between them cared for the children but I was always concerned to fill the larder and to leave clean changes of clothes. My feelings of guilt and apprehension were reserved for the lonely drives to and from the villages.

Year One 1955-56

Visitations – Term One
Entries in the log book for that first term record a succession of visits from those concerned with the affairs of the school. Never again would the village be so frequented; There were times in the years ahead when a visit from someone genuinely interested in the children and their work would have

been welcomed; but initial curiosity satisfied and a cursory report written, teachers were then left to continue in splendid isolation. Probably many preferred it to be so as opinions, advice and criticism from those outside the situation was often uninformed and irrelevant. Years later, Teachers' Centres were established in the towns and with the growing availability of cars – even for teachers – they provided the much needed opportunity for teachers to meet and discuss problems with those in similar situations.

Among those early visitors was the friendly and gossipy Inspector of Buildings who called frequently to assess repairs and internal decoration required for the building. The playground was a threat to all youngsters who took the inevitable tumble on its surface. Loose gravel, badly worn and scuffed, reduced our use of the area to a minimum. I had great ideas to extend the existing house garden into the adjoining half of the playground and to convert the gravelled waste into an area of lawns and shrubs and plots where we could grow flowers and vegetables. I tried very hard to convince Mr Sturgess that the extended garden would be of great benefit to us all, practically as well as aesthetically. I said that I would enlist the co-operation of parents to help with the maintenance and I think he was almost persuaded. Inevitably the initial cost of such an undertaking set against the cost of re-surfacing the area with asphalt decided the issue; and the procedure for laying the asphalt was simple and in accord with the established regulations for such work! At a later date he allowed me to order a goodly supply of paints used by a student to decorate the dreary expanse of wainscoting (more later) as a token to compensate for disappointment over the playground.

Miss S. was a great PE enthusiast and called repeatedly during that first term to ensure that I had ordered all the essential (in her opinion) equipment and to demonstrate how we could exercise indoors on bad days with the imaginative use of chairs! At that time there was an insistence that all the children should exercise in shirts and shorts for the obligatory twenty minute period physical exercise. In my opinion this was an unrealistic requirement for my varied group of pupils, and I was always apprehensive that she would arrive when we were exercising fully clothed. Lucky for me that the school was at least an hour's drive from Dorchester and that PE was timetabled for 10/15 each morning.

One of the more welcome visitors was RB her Majesty's Inspector for Dorset. We had met briefly in Germany when he, with the then Minister of Education and a small group of other HMI's came to visit the British Forces Educational Service set up in Germany after the war. They stayed in an hotel right next door to the multi-racial school started and organised by Audrey and myself in the pleasant town of Bad Salzuflen where all the embassies for the Allies were situated. We were suitably apprehensive at the thought of such prestigious visitors being our neighbours for a whole week but, in fact, it was a very enjoyable experience. They had come to observe and we had many informative and interesting discussions over teas and coffees. I remember that we were even wined and dined in the then renowned Bath Club by RB and one of his colleagues with talk of poetry, literature, music and everything under the sun – or moon rather – far into the night. RB then had been HMI for Cumbria and it was with some surprise when I realised he had transferred to Dorset by the time that I took over the school in Whitechurch. It was a very pleasant and reassuring surprise as there would be another in authority who would understand and support the principles on which our school functioned.

The interruptions to our daily routine continued. There were weekly visits from the Attendance man. (I think he had a more imposing title – an officer at least!) He came to check up on absenteeism but seemed to regard his chief function as that of confidant and advisor to the teacher. He was what would be considered as 'a fine upstanding figure of a man' in his middle years and no doubt thought of himself as a benevolent gift to all the single women teachers in isolation of the rural schools. His visits were always timed for the coffee or lunch breaks which he tried to prolong by relaying gossip and information from 'head office' and from other schools on his circuit. It was inevitable that I began to resent his patronage and his intrusion upon my hospitality and my valuable time. It seemed to me that his job was a sinecure and eventually I told him that I knew of all the circumstances when a pupil was absent for any length of time and that a visit from him would only cause trouble for me for having 'reported' the absence. I had a letter from 'head office' rebuking me for my lack of co-operation but the visits ceased, to my great relief.

I think that his role was another of those residual appointments from the past when the teacher's pay was based upon the number of pupils' attendances. The Register was sacrosanct and the daily ritual of calling each name and making the appropriate mark (black stroke for 'present' and red nought for 'absent') in the printed accuracy of the Register was still continued. It was checked by one of the Managers who would arrive unannounced and call out a few names at random to ensure that those marked 'present' were in fact not absent!

Mrs P. was one of the Managers whose self-appointed role was to check the register and she called for the first – and only – time to perform the ritual. I stood by thinking that she had used the performance as a reason for visiting and, when she had finished, I began to talk about the school and the funds which would be needed to supplement those from the LEA. I explained that I hoped for re-decoration of the old and dingy wainscot boarding and the equally dingy plaster of the high walls and roof. In my mind the list was endless but I just mentioned what I considered to be essential as I felt her withdrawal from my enthusiasm. She had just come to check the register, she explained. Was there any special reason I enquired, genuinely curious at the time? Her visit might well have coincided with one of the many days when I forgot the ritual and only made a cursory entry when there seemed to be a spare moment. There were additions of attendances to be computed vertically and horizontally at the end of each term and year – no doubt for some statistical information of which I was unaware – and the results were supposed to balance. It was a tedious and eye-straining exercise which seemed unnecessary as the figures were never asked for nor were they entered upon any of the official forms (few in those days!) and I soon 'forgot' to complete the formalities. When I asked if there was a special reason for her inspection of the register Mrs P. looked embarrassed. It had always been done, she said, and she thought it part of her responsibility as a Manager to conform. I asked if she ever conferred with the Attendance Officer about long-term absenteeism. (Boys were often absent for the weeks during hay-making and harvesting and I knew that two sisters were often kept at home by an ailing father to do the milking.) Evidently, there was no liaison between Managers and the LEA representative. I hastily changed the subject and tried to interest her in the new delivery of books. Mrs P. was a genteel lady 'interested in education' and was sensitive to this change in the regime and purpose of the village school and to the more professional attitude of its teacher. She never called again to check the register but gave me her support from a distance and over the occasional invitation for tea.

Library Books

The old order of the school as a Village Hall situation soon began to intrude into our daily work programmes and almost the first incident was concerned with the County Library books.

The elongated and worm-eaten cupboards and most of their contents were stacked at one end of the room with the old iron-clad desks waiting to be collected for disposal. The new stock was piled on makeshift shelving which would soon, with the aid of two helpful fathers, become the fixtures I had envisaged. A couple of wire-framed book stands had arrived and already the schoolroom had come to look more functional and workmanlike.

The small glass-fronted cupboard with its odd assortment of library books was left to be dealt with when – and if – a Library van should come to call. Its function became apparent one morning when an elderly person clad in a fur coat made her way through the room towards it. I was busy working with a group of children and did not immediately leave them to enquire her needs. She produced a couple of books from a bag and stood there in front of the cupboard. It was not locked and I wondered briefly why she did not open the door if she had come to return the books. She peered around the room, finally decided that I must be the teacher and came over.

'Miss Pearson always chose my books for me,' she announced in that not-of-the-village accent.

Then it would have to be after school hours, I said firmly; I

54

was busy and she could return at 4 o'clock. I had recognised her as living in a modernised cottage just down the road from the school and it would be no hardship for her to return later in the day. She persisted that Miss Pearson had always been ready to help whenever she called but I was equally insistent that I would only be available after school hours.

Later in the day I wrote a notice to state that Library books could be exchanged between 4pm and 5pm on one day in the week. Special arrangements could be made *if necessary*. And I pinned the notice to the outside door.

Harvest Festival

The good Canon was always sympathetic to my aims for the school and it was with some diffidence that he broached the subject of the Harvest Festival supper. He had seen my notice about the Library books and knew why it was there. However I assured him that I was well prepared. The Church choir and I were practising 'Sheep may safely graze' and the appropriate hymns. I had been shown the table set in the northern transept of the Church which would be heaped with produce brought by the children. The Canon would conduct a brief service for the children and any parents who cared to attend and I would play my recorder to accompany our rendering of ploughing the fields and scattering the good seed. All was under control, or so I thought.

'It's the Harvest Supper,' the Canon explained. It was always held in the schoolroom, he explained firmly as if he expected opposition. It would be held on a Friday to cause as little disruption as possible. I had no choice but to agree and co-operate. We would use the occasion as a centre of interest for collating a body of useful information... (farm produce, imported goods and their transport... endless forays into this 'seemless robe of knowledge'...) On the largest pieces of kitchen paper and wallpaper I could find I drew shapes of cornucopias from which spewed avalanches of labels, illustrations and cut-outs of all the wealth of goods with which our society is surfeited. The children of all ages – enjoyed collecting and arranging the material into groups according to content and into patterns suggested by shape and colour with much lively comment. I added my own comment in the form of an illustrated article on the work of Dr Schweitzer in Lambarene with the photo of an emaciated child prominently displayed.

The invasion started soon after 9am on the Friday in question while we were still hymn singing. For some reason the Canon was not there to take his usual weekly lesson with the older children. A van drew up outside the gates and a couple of men opened the door into the schoolroom announcing that they had brought the trestle tables. They were in a hurry – had work to do! So we dispersed while the trestles were stacked along the wall. I was told that they would be assembled later in the day. Comments and winks were directed at the older boys who were uncertain how to respond I was glad to note. I busied myself with the younger children trying to ignore the men and their cavalier attitude to the functions of the school – *their* school after all and some of the children must have been relatives. It had become daily more obvious that it would be a long haul before any degree of respect would be earned for the school and the 'school marm' who was employed there. Brawn rather than brain was still dominant in their scale of values. When Auntie Mary and myself removed the trestles on Sunday after Church to be ready for Monday morning school I wasn't too convinced that they could claim superiority in either respect!

Auntie Mary was hovering, anxious not to distract me but obviously in need of advice. Crates of crockery and dishes also had been left by the men but outside the small lobby which led into the adjoining room.

The children always used to unpack them she said apologetically. Already she had begun to realise that there was a change from the old casual practices which insidiously had been implemented during the recent years of the last teacher's illness. I compromised. The school dinners shortly would be delivered and the dining tables, on which the crockery was to be piled, were required for our own use. Those pupils who were willing could unpack the crates during the rest of the mid-day break. I could see that Auntie Mary was not too happy. The ladies would be coming shortly to make preparations for the feast and they would expect the crates to be unpacked, she said. There were at least six or seven hours before the supper was to start and I had understood that it consisted chiefly of cold meats, salads and 'spuds' which were cooked at the last minute in a nearby house. I was not prepared to encroach upon the school's scheduled work time unless it was absolutely necessary.

Auntie Mary often looked resigned at my demands upon her allegiance to the school and resignation closed upon her face as only two of the older girls (their mothers were among the helpers and there could have been recriminations) offered to help with the unpacking. She would be caught in the cross-fire of her allegiance to the past and the present in many future situations; but she became a true friend and ally, giving me her unstinted support in my efforts to re-establish the school as a centre of learning for the village children.

Through the window I caught a glimpse of her walking up the lane towards her home. Wise woman, I thought; so she was taking evasive action while the crocks were being unpacked with much crashing in the adjoining room.

Two large barrels of cider were the next to arrive, followed shortly after by trays of glasses brought over from the 'New Inn' on the further side of the crossroads.

We continued with our cornucopia collages and pinned them to the walls. (Was there any 'blu-tack' at the time? I only recall nails and drawing pins!) It was impossible to engage in any serious work so we relaxed with paints and crayons and a general talk about festivities and traditions. I was left in no doubt that the school was of very secondary importance to the use of the building as a village hall.

The reading room was much smaller and chiefly was used for afternoon meetings of the Women's Institute. I also learned, with some apprehension, that dances were often held in the schoolroom and that they were very popular, with coachloads coming from the surrounding villages. At least I had been warned!

During the afternoon the children and I stacked the new tables, desks and equipment at the far end of the room where I hoped it would all escape investigation by the curious. I would have to attend the supper and arranged to sit with members of the Church choir.

The children were dismissed when the men returned to put up the trestles. I waited while they did so, ostensibly to write up the daily diary of my work but in reality to assert my own authority in *my* workplace. The men worked speedily and with no adverse comments that I could hear... and the cornucopias were admired! I didn't care whether or not they liked me but I cared that they would *respect* me as the Headteacher of their school.

'Sorry to disturb you,' said one as they left. 'Have to get it done before milking.'

The ladies produced armfuls of white sheets and continued with the work of providing for over a hundred hungry and thirsty farmers and friends. They too needed to return home to feed children and to make their own preparations for the evening ahead. It was a spreadeagled kind of a village and many lived at a distance of one or two miles form the school so it was hoped that rain would not add to their difficulties. I sympathised.

It was a pleasant evening and despite my forebodings I enjoyed myself. Talk was of the weather, the harvest and local events. As tongues were loosened by the cider I heard favourable comments on the new desks and equipment; the 'shells' were pretty good too – and the Canon gave me a wink. No mention was made of the article on Dr Schweitzer; it was likely that he was unknown in that far corner of Dorset. The more boisterous behaviour of the men was kept in check by the presence of their women and of the Rector (his wife was an invalid and seldom appeared at village functions) and the Churchwardens. The supper ended by 9pm and I left to walk up the hill, past the row of council houses and along the narrow lane between hedges shadowed by the light from the seasonable harvest moon.

I felt warm and benevolent as I stopped in a gateway to look back upon my corner of this remote valley of the Dorset countryside. My eyes followed the line of lights from the council houses down to the crossroads. Lights still glimmered from the high, wide windows of the school and 'curtains', I thought again, curtains for warmth and protection on cold winter evenings as well as for protection against the fierce sunlight of summer days.

Would I be accepted? I wondered. Would my hopes and expectations for the school be realised? Miss W had said that it took at least twenty-five years for an outsider to be accepted by the villagers. Her father had been the Rector of the parish for ten years and she had lived in the village for twenty more years after his death and so felt she had earned the right to be buried in the Churchyard when the time came! But I was different, I thought; I had been born and bred and educated in Dorset and, eventually, had married a Dorset farmer. And yet, to identify too closely with the local farming community would pose its own problems. My place in the village would be ambiguous; my role as wife and mother would be difficult to equate with my role as a figure of authority in the minds of the parents for whose children I was responsible. Their confidence and acceptance would be hardly earned, I thought yet again.

A fox barked nearby and the moon hid behind a bank of clouds. Suddenly I was cold with apprehension as well as from the chill night air. What had I taken upon myself?

Interim

The term ended with the traditional preparations for Christmas although I would not be in the village during the Christmas period. The time had come to vacate the farmhouse and for the family's removal to the village of Whitechurch – only forty miles away but still a formidable undertaking.

The farm implements and cattle had been sold and the farm itself re-incorporated into the adjacent farm. In 1920 land belonging to a local landowner had been divided into three parts to provide three tenant farmers with small-holdings, two of which had reverted to a single tenancy in 1938. Now the original tenancy would be restored so ending a lifelong feud between the two families involved.

There had been no immediate urgency to vacate the farmhouse so that my husband and children had been able to stay there during that first term while I organised teaching and domestic arrangements in Whitechurch. Mrs Ashman had not yet left the village and, as my husband was now freed from the farmwork, between them the children were well cared for.

During the week I lived in the cottage which I was able to rent for the time that the work on the schoolhouse was in operation. I returned for the brief Christmas holiday to pack up personal possessions for the family and we all moved into the cottage before the start of the spring term. Such furniture which had not been sold was put into storage until the time when the renovations to the schoolhouse should be completed. I hoped that our temporary accommodation would be only for the term but the builders were a dilatory lot and we were not able to vacate the cottage until the summer holiday.

It was with some relief that the family was re-united and that I would not have to spend the weeks at the further end of the county with the cross country trek at weekends in that old Austin. We decided that Giles and Judith would not attend school until the summer term. They both needed to settle into their new surroundings and, as they both had colds, it was better not to take any risks, especially with Judith who was liable to develop bronchitis.

Also I was not yet established enough – or maybe energetic enough – to take on further commitments in the school. I knew that controversy over the use of the building as a Village Hall still had to be resolved and that the only justification for its primary use as a school would be in my ability to provide irrefutable evidence of the value of the school to the children. This inevitably would cause a few difficulties at first and I needed a breathing space for myself after all the demands of the past months. At least the move had achieved and I was optimistic enough to believe that school-and-family in unison would survive and flourish in this remote (then) corner of Dorset.

Second and third Terms

The Pantomime

There were signs that the schoolroom had been used in my absence during the Christmas holiday.

'A couple of meetings,' said Auntie Mary but she refrained from giving me any details and, at the time, I did not know her well enough to press for further information. Once again our own tables and chairs had been moved to one end of the room and again there was a pile of trestles stacked against two walls at the other end.

More interruptions... the struggle to reclaim the school was to continue.

The Canon already had advised me that there would be the annual production of a pantomime performed by the local amateur dramatic society of which he was an enthusiastic member. (I subscribe to the theory that an aptitude for acting is inherent in most parsons and teachers!) I asked Auntie Mary if she knew the proposed date of the production. She said that it would be in six weeks time and that the trestles would be erected as a stage. My immediate reaction was to ignore them and to restore the grouping of desks and tables throughout the whole length of the schoolroom. To confine the flexible groupings of pupils and work projects in a restricted space would necessitate a return to a more tightly controlled restriction of movement and sound. For example, singing and talking with the 5–7 year olds while older pupils were measuring and recording lengths, weights etc. while yet others were engaged upon writing a scene for the puppet theatre would be impossible to operate in the small space where the desks had been arranged... in rows!

Space... light... warmth... had been my requirements for a school building.

The stage area, marked out with chalk, seemed to take up an inordinate amount of pace and would effectively block access to the small room which I was beginning to use as an overspill from the big room for various activities. I was forced to compromise – to delay plans and projects until the production of 'Cinderella' (I think it was) should be over. For the next two months there would be a return to more formal work programmes which depended for the most part on pen/pencil and paper with myself giving as much individual help and tuition as possible. Back to talk-and-chalk method of teaching, I thought, with little opportunity for pupils to move from the confines of their desks. And it was still cold so that any possibility for going outside, even during the mid-day break, was limited. Flashes of memory recalled the ranged rows of desks to accommodate the 32 junior children in a room just fifteen feet square and other similar square rooms with larger desks to accommodate older (and larger) pupils in some of the city schools where I had taught and I was wryly grateful for having endured the experience. At least, in the present situation, the rows would soon be dispersed into more suitable groupings.

Those first weeks of my second term were a severe test of my endurance and restraint. There were constant comings and goings, hammerings and crashes as the stage was erected, arguments and parleys with a fine disregard for the school being conducted at the further end of the room. I think that many of the 'workers' were surreptitiously satisfying curiosity about the new teacher and verifying rumours concerning her unorthodox teaching methods. (They would be disappointed in the latter having imposed a return to the narrow system of their own early experiences of school.)

On the Friday morning, according to custom, the Vicar arrived to take the morning service followed by a Scripture lesson with the older pupils. We were singing a hymn when a portion of the stage collapsed. The Vicar decided to retreat but he must have intervened on our behalf as, after that first week, the daily intrusions almost ceased. Rehearsals and further constructions were restricted to evenings and weekends. I was thankful at this time that we were *not* occupying the schoolhouse. At a later date we were to suffer from disturbance and noise when, at the insistence of the Managers and a new Vicar, dances were held in the schoolroom. (More anon.)

The pantomime was performed by a small group of would-be singers and play-actors who, no doubt, enjoyed their performances rather more than their audiences. However, their efforts were well supported and I accompanied the children for a matinee rendition at the weekend. But it was a great relief when it was all over, the stage and its trimmings were dismantled and we could once again spread ourselves in comfort and with freedom from the restrictions we had endured.

We were soon busy with out own end-of-term Springtime Celebration of dance and song, readings and recitations in a room bright with garlands and posies of Spring flowers and Easter gardens made by the children to take home after the concert.

The family

I knew that my husband and the children were the subject of curiosity and speculation. They were now living in the rented cottage at some distance from the school and had only been seen casually by a few. I had referred to them in conversation when it had seemed suitable to do so and a Sunday morning Church service provided a good opportunity to present them formally. Heads were turned as we made our entry to take out seats near the back of the Church and, after the service, we stood by the Vicar while he made the introductions.

The following Sunday I left them in their seats while I took my usual place in the choir stalls. Judith had been distracted by my husband while I left them but, during the first hymn, she suddenly saw me. Judith always had a mind of her own despite her disability and, before her father was aware, she was trotting down the length of the aisle to join me. The chancel steps proved to be a deterrent and I had to rescue her and take her with me into the stalls. From that Sunday onwards both Judith and Giles sat with me in the choir stalls to avoid any further distractions for the congregation.

It became obvious that I would have to 'introduce' Giles and Judith to the children before they actually came to school. To talk about Giles was easy; he was the same age as young Tony but his name was unfamiliar until I explained that it was the same as in 'farmer Giles' because his father had been a farmer. This was understood although 'Charles' frequently was substituted for 'Giles'.

Judith was something else... she had a handicap. Philip had a handicap as he wore a calliper on his right leg after an operation on a t.b. hip; John had a handicap – he stammered badly; Brian had a handicap – his eyesight was poor and at the time he wore a patch over one side of his spectacles. Most people had handicaps of one sort or another at sometime in their lives – and I listened to a whole litany of handicaps among those known to the children! I said that handicaps could not always be seen, that the brain itself could be damaged or faulty in some way which could affect a person's behaviour. And I told them of Judith and that she would attend the school just as anyone else

63

with a handicap would do so. I'm sure that this was followed by a homily on the need to tolerate and help those less fortunate than ourselves. (Mrs Lennox, the teacher who was to join me in my fourth year, always told me that I had a tendency to preach!)

I said that she and Giles would join us the following term. There came the day when they were entered on the register. Giles was never happy about accepting the duality of my role as mother and teacher and it became evident that transfer to another village school in the locality was advisable. Contrary to expectations Judith fitted into our small community with no difficulty. She was always an imitator and parodied the learning – and teaching! – gestures to perfection – when she felt so inclined. She found a great friend in Josie who was a slow learner and the two of them would make great efforts to emulate the achievements of others in their 'group'. There was so much that they *could* do; none more dashing than they with paints and crayons! Josie progressed slowly with reading and number work and Judith managed to 'read' mechanically (for example, by memorising a few pages from the 'Janet and John' reading scheme.)

Judith often provided much welcomed light relief during some of the more serious and onerous sessions in which sometimes we were engaged. I remember one incident quite clearly. The scene was morning assembly when I was engaged in one of my homilies. The adjoining door to the cloakroom opened and Judith appeared garbed in a selection of clothes she had taken from the hooks; a boy's cap set rakishly over her plaits completed the spectacle. She stood there expectantly while we all gaped at the vision finally dissolving into gusts of laughter. Later on she had a penchant for 'finding' sandwiches and snacks brought by children who did not have school dinners and she would take these to feed some hens kept in an enclosure just down the road. I soon learned to keep a tin of sandwich meat in store – just in case! There were other incidents through the years when she attended the school and they were always tolerated with amusement and affection and I was never aware of any resentment or hostility towards her from the other children. I'm sure that she would have left me in no doubt had there been any animosity shown to her.

Then it was summer with warm days which allowed us to

work in the garden. With a tea trolley rescued from a jumble sale to transfer books, paints and other necessities; and the home-made clip-boards, excursions for the varying groups to the garden became an acceptable part of our routine. I daresay that 'time was wasted' by some but, on the whole, assignments of work were completed and progressed according to my detailed schemes of preparation and forecasting. Where better on a summer's day to hear Guy read his account of a walk on Hardown Hill, or myself to read an excerpt from Tolkein's 'Lord of the Rings' while coloured threads stitched patterns on canvas and sacking and younger fingers busied themselves with exploring possibilities of adding to their wormery.

Sports Day

Our sports day helped to draw our small community together and, traditionally, had always been held on the Vicarage lawn – weather permitting. It shared with the annual Church Fete the doubtful privilege of trampling the lawn and intruding into the Vicarage kitchen and I sympathised with the Vicar and his wife for the disruption of *their* privacy and property. Also – traditionally- buns and tea were provided by the Vicar and the Squire – if one should be available. I must admit to the occasional spasm of envy when I heard of strawberries and cream being provided for the schoolchildren by the Squire's wife in a neighbouring village, although I'm sure that I'd have responded badly to the patronage!

To think of a sports day in a conventional way made no sense at all with 19 children varying so diversely in every way. Even with handicaps (and who would determine what and how?) the old favourites such as egg-and-spoon, sack races and team events made the winning-with-prizes aspect of the activities inappropriate. I could well imagine the comments of 'not fair', 'he cheated', (what will we not do to win?) 'not fair'. And of course, it wouldn't be fair, it *couldn't* be fair. So it had to be fun and, like the caucus race in Alice, *everyone* had to win, everyone had to be encouraged to win. With those mothers who could spare the time to meet after school we devised a programme of events, partly based on the old familiar races but with variations

65

to ensure that all had a fair chance to win a prize. We limited the amount of prizes any one child could collect to three. After that, the winner would be asked to forego the prize in favour of the next competitor. It was easy to devise fun games with the use of quoits, balls, hoops and ropes and with the addition of all kinds of household goods for creating 'obstacles' and 'targets'. For the older pupils we agreed there had to be a high jump, the long jump, sprint relays and so on. And those 19 children were divided –by me – into groups of 3's, 4's and 5's according to age, size and comparable ability; and according to *my* judgement; if there had to be a competitive element let it be seen by pupils and parents to be as 'fair' as possible.

I well remember Chris, a heavily built girl of 11 years who would never win any prize and who might well have been made to look – and feel- awkward and stupid. She had a special prize for helping me to hold one end of the finishing rope and to gather up abandoned quoits, eggs, etc. Her help was invaluable and her 'special' role was much appreciated by her elderly parents. Parents often feel a child's 'failure' more acutely than the child as I realised when the dreaded 11+ results were publicised.

At a much later date I took a group of pupils to a Sports Day at a Centre for the mentally handicapped. It was an inspiration to see those with every kind of handicap enjoying the occasion and making tremendous efforts to join in all the events, events which were 'tailored' to accommodate the diversity of handicaps by an inspired and dedicated teacher. (Judith was to be a pupil there when she was 11 years old.)

The mothers and I devised the detailed programme, praying that rain would not spoil the day, and copies were made by the pupils (handwriting practice!) for every family. Buns and tea were to be augmented by a lavish provision of sandwiches, cakes, squash and ice-cream for the competitors and tea would be provided for the parents. It was also decided to limit the use of the Vicarage kitchen to boiling a kettle for the tea, a concern much appreciated by the Vicar's wife!

That first year the sun shone and the afternoon was enjoyed by us all. I felt a glow of satisfaction as I watched the children enjoying their well-earned tea while parents grouped and gossiped over their tea. A table of 'glittering prizes' held a collection of baubles and sweets (I regret to say) collected and given by hard-pressed mothers and there was a splendid prize-giving by the Vicar before we all dispersed. Everyone had at least one prize – none more than the three stipulated – which I judiciously handed to the Vicar to pass on as the names were called.

Sports Day signified the end of the summer term and the end of my first year as the new teacher of the village school. It was difficult to evaluate what progress had been made in my aim to restore its rightful place as a centre of scholastic activity in the village. Four pupils from the 'top' group had passed the 11+ for entry to the Grammar School and this had helped to establish confidence in my (then) unorthodox teaching methods. I had come to know each and every one of those 19 children and most of their backgrounds so that I was able to plan work schedules with more accurate reference to individual difficulties and interests. I had six weeks in which to make all the detailed preparations for the year ahead.

It was now possible to move from the rented cottage into the schoolhouse. The workmen finally had finished earlier in the term but there was still work to be done after they had left. My husband was able to do the decorating and to build a fuel bunker. A bathroom had been added built on supports and with access at the top of the stairs. My husband enclosed the space beneath with a structure of breeze blocks and glass. It resembled a signal box but it kept the north winds from penetrating the one door which led directly into the sitting room; and, as the house was built along the back wall of the school, it was not visible from the road. The septic tank in the field opposite functioned and it was wonderful to have a flush toilet. There were also three flush toilets for the girls and another for the boys. I had a Rayburn cooker (a cheaper version of an Aga) installed in the kitchen which heated water for the bathroom. Central heating with radiators was beyond the limits of the expenditure allowed. However, by comparison with privies, makeshift baths and kettles of hot water, the new plumbing provided every comfort.

Our furniture came out of store and several trips transported our belongings from the cottage. All and every move was scrutinised by Mrs M. from the New Inn at the crossroads. Later in the day she brought me a cabbage from her garden. I thought it was a gift but she said that it was cheap at price she asked! I had no doubt that a full description of our meagre household would be relayed in the bar later in the day.

The following weeks were busy with putting everything in order. We enjoyed days by the sea when the weather allowed. The beach at Charmouth was still quiet and unspoilt. I had always loved the sea and swimming and it provided a wonderful escape from the daily demands of work and family. My husband often preferred to stay at home but Giles and Judith shared with me the joys of beach and sea.

Those few weeks were a pleasant interlude with days lived leisurely and my evenings spent in the schoolroom preparing the year ahead.

Getting Established

My credentials as a 'good' teacher had been established when Sylvia, Felicity, Sonia, Robert, Guy and Harry all passed the 11+ hurdle for entry to the Grammar School during those first two years. At the time I was grateful for the selection tests as the 'successes' offset the suspicions about my teaching methods – with no rigidly timetabled 'lessons', with subjects diffused into projects; and 'classes' dispersed into fluctuating groups. There was also my even less orthodox family background.

Judith had established her own niche with Jo and Leslie whom I would have to 'train' rather than 'educate' in the years ahead. Giles did not settle. Since the age of four I had been for him both Mother and Teacher. He was almost seven when we moved to Whitechurch and, as a lively and mischievous child he was an easy target to blame for any minor misdemeanours committed by others.

My husband also was somewhat of an enigma. He did not associate with the local farmers, seemed to have no particular hobbies or interests. The Vicar tried to involve him in some of the affairs of the Church but he was not interested. He worked occasionally on an estate in the nearby village but for most of the time he read and was addicted to the television.

How different was this mix of a family from my predecessors who had lived in the schoolhouse, all single or married without children and all 'respectable' fitting the stereotyped image of the schoolteacher. I thought of myself as a professional, committed to the work for which I had been appointed; and with my private life of no concern to anyone but myself. How many others in public life, wherever on the scale of importance in the community, have suffered from the same illusion. And, in a village, we lived under the microscope of local curiosity and censure.

I was convinced that my competence as a teacher and my allegiance to the Church should offset any inadequacies in my private life. I underestimated the impact that my unorthodox role as breadwinner with an unemployed husband made upon the entrenched traditional male dominance in the village. However, I had the full support of the Vicar and the approval of three of the Managers when they saw the changes in the work and behaviour of the children. Without their support during those first two years my uphill struggle to establish the school as a centre of learning and 'enlightenment' might well have faltered. Only during the hours when I was actively involved with the pupils in the schoolroom was I able to divorce myself from demands of husband and family; the work so often was the remedy for periods of personal doubts and anxieties.

The Fire

The lovely old farmhouse was – and still is – a few hundred yards along the road from the school and Giles often went there to play with the son of the farmer. They were about the same age although the son went to a private school following his family's tradition.

One Saturday morning my telephone rang; did I know that there was a fire in the village not far from the school? The smoke could be seen from a house up the hill. I had a premonition – where was Giles? I hurried out into the road down towards the farm.

The fire was in the historic tythe barn adjacent to the house. The barn was built on two levels and with a thatched roof. Smoke was pouring from the open hatchway on the upper level. Scorched pigs and hens were escaping from the ground floor on to the road. The smell of burning flesh and acrid smoke was pervasive.

I was left in no doubt what had happened. A small crowd had gathered already. It was my son who had bought the matches from the small post office/shop. He, with the farmer's son and another boy had been playing cowboys in the upper level of the barn and had made a camp fire which had set light to the bales of hay stored there. A passer-by had seen a trail of smoke coming from the hatchway and had alerted the farmer's wife. The fire had flared quickly and she had only just enough time to climb the ladder and throw down the three terrified boys before the thatch caught and began to fall in burning chunks into the space where they had been playing.

There were murmurs as I made my way to the farmhouse. They – the farmer and his wife – wouldn't want to see me; I'd be better employed at home looking after my children... the hostility was evident. The farmer and his wife were more than kind. The boys were alright and Giles had run to the Vicarage for refuge. The fire engine was on its way. I was reassured that the barn was fully insured and I was also told – in confidence – that they had been trying to get a new purpose-built barn to replace the old but that the tythe barn was a protected building of historic interest. I was not sure if this was said to give me some comfort but I was more than grateful for their consideration.

Giles had been badly scared but the kindly Canon had given him drinks and a bun and then walked back with us to the schoolhouse. We were met by Auntie Mary with Judith. News of the fire had quickly spread. She had been on her way to the school when she saw me running down the road, had used her great fund of common sense and had taken care of Judith.

We went to Church the following day and it was school again on Monday. I had a talk with the Vicar – my husband was away at the time – and I made another of those momentous decisions; that Giles should go as a boarder to a preparatory school. His friend also was going to a boarding school although, for some reason, not the same one. It was against my political and educational principles but at the time there seemed to be no alternative.

In subsequent years it often seemed a heartless decision to have sent him away to school at such a young age; but fashions of thought on child rearing and education come and go and, at the time, private education in such a school was considered to be a privilege. He had not settled at all well in the Charmouth School and I began to see more problems arising from his continued attendance there. The cost of sending him to Clayesmore was financially crippling on a teacher's salary and with little input from my husband; but there seemed to be no

71

alternative.

'We do the best we can in the circumstances in which we find ourselves,' I have often told Giles in later years when he has told me how much he resented being sent away from home.

Eventually, at the age of 13 years, with a recommendation from the Education Officer, he was transferred to the boarding Grammar school in Beaminster. From there he was able to come home at weekends when he felt the need. He made friends and was there until he left at the age of 17 years to join the Merchant Navy.

The continued absence of my husband, the fire, and even Judith's unpredictable escapades undermined the tenuous confidence in my suitability as the village schoolteacher. However, no actual complaint was made and no children were withdrawn from the school.

And the school continued to flourish

The schoolroom itself looked organised and purposeful. The old cupboards had been replaced by shelving on which were displayed books and models, simple musical instruments and whatever was of interest at the time. We even had a piano begged from the LEA. There was the nucleus of our museum started by the donation of a lovely conch shell by a well-wisher and the dried snake-skin found by one of the children; and we were adjacent to the geographical stratum of blue lias rich in fossils. Our collection of ammonites and tribolites would have been the envy of many busy with their hammers and collecting bags in later years.

The old iron-clamped desks had been replaced by serviceable flat-topped tables – so good for grouping to form a stage (covered with my bedroom carpet!) and small tables which could so easily be re-arranged as the need arose. The walls had been cleaned and colour-washed; a pleasant pinkish mushroom colour replaced the old traditional yellow with dark-green wainscoting. Folk-weave curtains softened the large bare windows and shaded the room from summer suns and winter gales. Mobiles (paste and paper were put to a dozen uses!) hung from the beams and couple of good prints (changed periodically) shared space on the walls with the children's own work.

School dinners were brought in containers from Lyme Regis. Four long trestle tables were prepared by Auntie Mary in the small adjacent room and meal was shared by staff and children together. Often I would play a record on my daughter's wind-up gramophone; I remember that an aria from the opera 'Orpheus in the Underworld' was a favourite – accompanied of course by the story – and others – from the old Greek myths. The meal was essentially a social event and there was always time for chatter and talk as well. Auntie Mary shared it all with us and was invaluable in helping the young ones when required. The hour always sped by so easily; how different from the nightmare dinner duties in halls trying to control hungry and bored children waiting in lines to be served and then having to find a place where the half-cold food could be eaten – a constant reminder of institutions and charitable provision for the 'lower orders' of our society.

Even on a superficial level it was impossible to ignore the up-grading of the school by even the most prejudiced of my critics. Their children – and grandchildren – were daily in my care and subject to my influence. I really had the advantage, and knew it, although at the time I often felt depressed by the antagonism and by the occasional opposition to the changes I wished to make.

The building was surrounded by an area of gravel and this in turn was divided by a low stone wall which, in the past, had served to separate the girls from the boys. The only access from one side to the other was through the schoolroom. We needed the space that removal of the stone wall would provide and I applied to the Managers to have this done. I could not believe that there would be any objection as the days when the school was an 'all-through' school for pupils aged 5-14 years and it was thought proper for the boys (and their urinal) to be kept separate from the girls, were long past. But there was objection; the wall symbolised another of those changes the teacher was making to the established order familiar to several from their own years as pupils in the school.

Eventually the wall *was* demolished but I was always careful not to mention the obvious advantages. I had tried to

73

persuade the LEA to replace the gravel with lawns and shrubs and areas for the children to cultivate but in this I had been defeated by the long arm of officialdom. To this day I still hate the arid stretches of asphalt – even in car parks! Luckily there was a well-maintained garden which belonged to the schoolhouse and which was used by us all.

I knew that I had the support of many of the mothers, several of whom secretly sympathised with my family problems – they had their own in that male dominated community! They joined in enthusiastically with all the money-raising projects and with the many other activities where extra help was always needed.

***

There were changes ahead to which I would have to accommodate. Our good friend the Canon was far from well and decided that he would have to retire in the near future. The death of Miss W. and the retirement of Mrs P. as School Managers left two vacancies in our governing body. I had asked two of the mothers who already were active in the support of the school if they would consider being elected. The position had always been one of patronage rather than of involvement and I knew that representatives from the parents would not easily be acceptable by the other parents. However, the people's Church warden – a Manager by virtue of his office – was also the father of three girls in the school so that there was a precedent – however skewed! I talked it over with the Vicar and the two mothers were appointed. It was not an easy role for them and often their loyalties to the school and to myself were put under strain. Other parents, especially mothers, were jealous until I suggested that there would be a change every two years and that anyone interested should apply to the vicar.

Their role differed from that of their predecessors. I could not confide in them to the same extent that I had found to be so helpful during my first year in the village. But they *were* a great help in a practical way and were more obviously a part of the school life than had been the custom – helping to make Christmas cakes and puddings instead of checking the register!

74

Gradually we were becoming a more democratic community and this in a village where divisions of class were firmly upheld by the inhabitants and enforced by the incoming residents who formed their own social groups apart from the local families.

Student Apprentice

When the small private school in Charmouth was closed six of the pupils transferred to our village school. They were all aged 8-11 years, lively and used to individual tuition. They were a welcome addition to my 'top' group whom I particularly enjoyed teaching but I became hard-pressed to give enough time and attention to the younger children. I discussed my misgivings with the visiting Inspector who suggested that the appointment of a student could be of benefit to both of us. He knew of a pupil who was about to leave the Grammar school and who hoped to train as a teacher but was uncertain about entering College so soon after leaving school.

Daphne came for a year and, after a few shaky starts, was indispensable. Eventually she devised her own programmes of work with the middle group while I was able to concentrate on working with the older pupils and with the very young ones who had to be led gently into the skills of talking, reading and numeracy. Daphne was lively, imaginative and worked with the zest and energy of youthful enthusiasm. She was a great favourite with all the children and especially with Judith who would call out 'Catcham' (a distortion of 'Matcham' Daphne's surname) from wherever she happened to be in order to gain Daphne's attention. It was always 'Miss Matcham' by us all in school to assert her status as another teacher. She was paid by the LEA as an uncertificated teacher which helped her finances when she went to College. She lived at home in Lyme Regis and energetically cycled the five miles to and from school.

She left a permanent record of her stay with us by painting a mural on the dreary wooden wainscoting at one end of the schoolroom. With many willing helpers scenes from familiar fairy tales and nursery rhymes transformed the old woodwork into a colourful and useful display area for the younger children.

I remember that a hole in the woodwork was disguised as the entry into a mountain where the Pied Piper led a band of gaily dressed and laughing children. We were all very sad to see her leave although we knew that she would often return when time permitted.

For her part she said that the year's experience in our small school was of enormous help when she went to College. She was able to relate the theory to her own practical experience and was able to participate more fully in the organised associations with local schools. I know that she became an able and valued teacher and I often think that the old apprenticeship system of initiation into a career has much to commend it.

The following year two first-year students from the College were allocated to our school for three weeks teaching experience. They stayed in lodgings during the week and returned to College at the weekends. This was not a successful exercise.

It takes time to become involved with the work and life of a school and especially in a school with a flexible timetable and with programmes of work which were so often in need of revision and change. Much of my own precious time was spent in helping the students to prepare and organise suitable work with the children in my so-called 'middle' group and the sessions after school put a strain on my physical and nervous resources. They were an ill-matched pair and both missed the communal life of the College. Two visits from the College tutor were of little help and further disrupted our work and equilibrium! I wrote to the College and to my friend in the LEA suggesting that one student for the period of least a whole term was the only system of school experience which could be of benefit to the children, the student and myself. After further discussion with the visiting tutor – an expensive visit in time and petrol – the decision to give students experience in remote country schools was cancelled.

Years later when I was a College tutor in Liverpool and Northampton the problem of a system in which a student spent two or three weeks in a school at any one time was often discouraging and wearisome – a period to be endured rather than enjoyed. There were so many variables to be considered when placing a student with a group of children for such brief – and disconnected – periods of time that such placements were often perfunctory rather than calculated by the tutor in charge.

A whole year attached to a school – or even to a maximum of three schools before entry to College where courses are biased towards academic study would seem to be more beneficial to all concerned. Since the introduction of the B.Ed. degree course for teachers the revision of such courses in the Colleges – now re-graded as Universities – has been constant.

A Second Teacher

As the number of pupils crept upwards towards forty it became obvious that the permanent appointment of a second teacher was necessary. It was with some reluctance and apprehension that I made a request to the LEA for the appointment of a teacher who would be responsible for the younger children. I knew that my own temperament and abilities did not accord with the usual formalities of a daily routine and that often activities and emerging interests would cut across the timetable and age groups. Our 'concerts' and projects were like collages incorporated into the warp and weft of our ongoing programmes. Another teacher could put restrictions upon my freedom to disrupt routines, my freedom to make judgements and decisions. And yet, another teacher with whom to exchange ideas, concerns and propositions for the children and their work could be a great asset to us all. *But* she would need to be flexible and would need to share my own convictions about teaching and living in this small community of learning.

Eventually the post was advertised and I was allowed to stipulate that there would be a trial period of at least one year for each of us. If there was no 'fit' I would be prepared to wait and to continue with long-term student placements.

How lucky I was! There were only two applicants and E.L. was the obvious choice. Her teaching experience had been with young children in a Lancashire country school. She had moved to Dorset with a colleague after the untimely death of her husband. She was just two years older than myself and immediately we began to talk of the frustrations and disadvantages for both teachers and pupils of working in the large institutionalised large schools where the children are divided by age into the one-yearly classes. I explained that we would share the large classroom between us – with no dividing screen – but that the so-called 'dining' room could be used more often as a workroom for each of us when required.

There was never any problem. We worked amicably together for the next eight years and until the threat of closure sent me off on a year's course to Bristol and from there to teach in a Liverpool College. E.L. was a great support through all the vicissitudes yet in store for us. It was so 'right' from the very start. We complemented each other's specific interests, her's in Maths, and mine in Language. She was so good with the younger children which released me to carry the older children on my own flights of fantasy! We worked together in the same room occasionally divided by our home-made movable screens and with interchanges of space and pupils as the needs arose.

For me it was a great relief to have someone with whom to discuss the daily affairs of the children, their families and the community in which we lived. She walked the two miles to school each day from the village where she shared a pleasant home with another teacher friend. She, with Auntie Mary and myself, were the lynch pins on which the school functioned, each with her own separate and distinctive role and each indispensable to the well-being of everyone concerned.

It seemed to me then – and since – that this was a near-ideal situation in which teachers and all involved with the education of young children could best be of service to the whole community.

Changes

The time passed swiftly as our routine of work was established and with school and Church closely involved with the ongoing activities and concern in the village. The schoolroom looked busy and functional and was used only for meetings during the holidays. It would have been almost impossible to have stored books and apparatus and project work for safe keeping; the two large cupboards used by my predecessor for such purposes had long since been disposed of. A large marquee was hired and erected in the small field adjacent to the Reading Room for the annual flower show and the R.R. also was used for reduced productions by the Amateur Dramatic Society. The school once again was restored as a centre of learning in the village and had achieved a semblance of the vision I had formed in my mind when first I had stood in that dilapidated building wondering whether or not to apply for the post as Headteacher.

But changes were imminent; continuing changes in Educational theories and practices, social changes in the structure of the village community and changes in my own personal circumstances.

Education

'Go slowly,' I had been advised but teachers themselves were under pressure. The language of 'what' and 'how' and 'why' of what was being taught in the schools began to burgeon with a whole new vocabulary included in theories designed to infuse the scholastic system with new impetus and wider directions. The limited curriculum was extended to include introductory courses in science, physics, biology, a second language, dance/drama and physical education (not just physical training). The emphasis on the verification of 'facts' eroded content and methodology of such subjects as history and geography. (How do you know that you know? became the slogan for harassed teachers!)

Batteries of evaluative and diagnostic tests devised by the Educational Psychologists were introduced to replace subjective judgements and analyses of children's work and attainments. These were to provide statistical evidence of learning progress and to indicate problem areas; but also to reflect the competence – or otherwise – of the teachers.

The confidence derived from the practice of known and tried procedures and routines for many older teachers was undermined by the bombardment of such radical and wide-sweeping challenges to the established order of their careers. There were breakdowns; there were exits into more rewarding and less stressful forms of employment; and there were resistances to any suggestion of change. My own early enthusiasm and confidence were curbed and chastened by these winds of change even though I was often in agreement with the new insights into the 'what' and 'how' of my work with the children. Such concepts as open-plan organisation, group teaching, ability grouping, child-centred education with the emphasis on *learning* rather than *teaching* and learning through direct experience (Piaget's 'concrete operations') were self-evident ways of educating children in the village school situation. It was unfortunate that such theories and procedures were often imposed in the institutionalised schools with disastrous results for the children and teachers alike. There is no uniform blueprint to prescribe how children learn or how they are to be taught. There are too many variables in locality and size of the school and in the individual characteristics of children and teachers to make such uniformity possible – thank goodness!

My own teaching methods did not concur with the formal instruction with which the parents were familiar. No chanting of arithmetic tables was to be heard through the open windows; no formal drill exercises at regular times in the playground were to be seen. Instead, children in ones or twos could be observed outside the school unsupervised (as it seemed!) measuring, drawing and occupied with activities unrelated to 'lessons'. However, we were a Church school, and I conformed to the expectations registered by the Church calendar. We made Easter gardens; we sang on the Church tower for Ascension day (mothers included to help the younger ones up the stone stairway!); we made our contributions at Harvest Festival; and Christmas was a feast of shepherds, kings and a manger scene. I also took charge of the Church choir for a weekly practice in the Church or in the school as I had been able to persuade the LEA to provide us with the re-conditioned piano.

During those first two years confidence in me as a teacher gradually became confirmed when pupils were accepted for further education at the Grammar school in Lyme Regis.

Social

The texture of the village was changing. Farm workers, made redundant by the increasing use of farm machinery, left the village to find work elsewhere. Cottages and even farms were bought, modernised and extended to meet the requirements of the new inhabitants. These consisted of three main groups: the elderly retired from nearby towns; ex-colonial service families with children at independent boarding schools; and comparatively affluent families with transport for commuting to work who also sent their children to fee-paying schools. With very few exceptions none of them were interested in the village school.

However, there *were* exceptions. We welcomed for time two sisters and their young brother, children of an Airforce officer and his wife who were stationed in the area; and two other sisters, daughters of a local business man. It was good to have a social mix in the school and a great help in my efforts to develop clear articulation and use of language with all the children. In a dozen ways it was obvious that families who spoke with a slurred Dorset accent were not included in the affairs of this recent infiltration into the village.

The separation of 'them' and 'us' was to become even more emphasised with the appointment of a new Vicar, an ex RAF officer, after the retirement and eventual death of our kindly Canon. He identified with the newcomers and had little interest in the school or the children; his own two sons had been to

81

Independent schools. One of my own pupils said to me years afterwards, 'We're good enough to clean the Church but not to have any say in the affairs of the Church.' It was sad to hear that the social structure of the village had changed so little over a distance of thirty years. All our efforts to promote a democratic and inter-related social mix in the school and the village had disappeared with the final closure of the school.

I wrote a poem at the time which it seems appropriate to include as it describes quite clearly the break-up of the established structure of the village – and that of many other similar villages at the time.

Disintegration

The inter-plaiting of nylon threads
with coarser homespun of village weave
unravels the basic pattern; breeds
discordant jangles past reprieve.

The interplay of sophist minds
that overbid the slurring thoughts
and grated speech of country kind
impose with ease their smooth-tongued cult.

They take the rough and knotted grain
of homespun cloth and cut the threads
to suit their own conversions; spin
their own designs and alien creeds
upon the straining warp, which frays
and breaks: unravelling quickly spreads
the village now a jangled maze
of disconnected separate threads.

(1968)

In many ways I resented the intrusion and yet in other ways I could appreciate that the infusion of new blood into the hardened cement of habit and tradition could be of benefit to the school and to myself as a person. I too had been an intruder into an established pattern of village life. Children from two of the 'new' families joined our school. School fees for private education were high and approval for the work being achieved in our village school already was gaining recognition. The four children of different ages fitted easily into the social and learning ethos of the school but I had to be diplomatic in my relationships with the parents. They themselves were well educated and were ambitious for their children's advancement. I welcomed their interest in our work but was careful always to involve *all* parents in our activities and talks in and out of school hours. It was often difficult to maintain the balance between their involvement and my own professional judgements related to the ongoing programmes of work and the function of the school in the village situation. Their own loyalties to the school were to be strained in the near future.

Managers Meetings were held at irregular intervals to discuss the use of the schoolroom apart from its educational function. Matters of finance and repairs to the building were the usual subjects on the agenda and occasionally matters arising from complaints by parents or staff. Appointments of the teacher(s), the caretaker and the meals supervisor were the more responsible decisions undertaken by the Managers. It was not mandatory but a courtesy for the Headteacher to be invited to the meetings; to be excluded was tantamount to an expression of disapproval and criticism of the teacher concerned. I had always been invited! And it was in such a situation that the two new parent/managers found themselves when, at a later day, financial support for the building reached a crisis under the Chairmanship of the new Vicar.

Changes in the village did not immediately affect the ongoing work in the school and we continued to flourish. With the appointment of a second teacher my own work load became easier. There was no national curriculum and pressures from external 'authorities' were restricted to occasional visits from the H.M.I. (Her Majesty's Inspector) and one or two advisors from the LEA, visits which we welcomed in order to discuss topics of interest related to our work with the children. The imperative to train children in literacy and numeracy was implicit in all our daily affairs, in our enjoyment of stories, puzzles, making-and-

83

doing. There was so much more to 'education' than 'training'. There were concerts and celebrations in dance and song, readings and recitations, seeing patterns in nature which was all around us, making our own patterns with words and shapes and colours, collecting and classifying for our Museum, learning to collaborate and to work alone. The days were full and enjoyable.

The Rev. Syers and his wife arrived in the village during the early part of the year 1958. I think it was March and during the Easter holiday I invited them both for tea in the schoolhouse. Mrs Lennox was also present and I had arranged for Giles and Judith to stay with friends so that there would be no interruptions to the introductions. The event was all very formal and I soon realised that neither the new Vicar nor his wife had any interest in the village school. Afterwards Mrs Lennox said that I had been too enthusiastic!

No return invitation to the Vicarage was ever received!

However Rev Syers did agree that Friday mornings would be suitable for him to take a short service in the school and to give a half hour's instruction to the older pupils.

He came reluctantly and infrequently. He told me that he suffered from migraine and I sympathised. I appreciated that it wasn't easy for him to come for his weekly visit into the semi-formality of our school and to instruct young children with whom he had little or no rapport. His life of authority in the Air Force had been completely different from that of initiating young children into the rituals of religious doctrine. Eventually I suggested – tactfully I hope – that I was quite prepared to take over the Friday morning commitment as I realised that teaching young children wasn't an easy undertaking especially as he only met them for a brief period once a week. In fact it would have been much easier for all of us had he agreed; quite often the uncertainty of his infrequent visits were disruptive to all of us.

Unfortunately he interpreted my suggestion as a criticism. He said nothing at the time but weeks later I received a note from the Vicarage stating that as I was not satisfied with his visits they would not therefore be resumed. The limited but essential communication between the Vicarage and the school was to continue on this formal exchange of written memos.

The new Vicar grouped around him the more recent arrivals

in the village who gradually took over the Church duties and activities. The political implications of this social change in the village could not be ignored. The Vicar and his supporters revived the old hierarchical superiority of the Church as in Victorian times.

There was no Chapel in the village where dissenters could establish a more democratic community of worship and fellowship. Gradually the school became the centre for local families, a focus for other ways of conducting relationships and activities than those centred around those who could spare time and money for their social indulgences. I had withdrawn from the choir, which had been taken over by ladies with more musical knowledge and expertise than myself but continued to sit in the body of the Church with the rest of the congregation. A further incident at the Harvest Festival made my separation from the Church activities rather more obvious.

It had been the custom always for us to decorate with our gifts of vegetables, fruit and flowers a table set in the northern transept opposite the wide southern entrance door. The new Vicar asked me if the children would please leave their gifts in the porch as the ladies who were in charge of decorating the Church knew best how to display them to their advantage. I said that 'no', I couldn't possibly ask the children to do this. We would hold the Harvest Festival celebrations in our school. The usual gifts from farms and gardens were heaped upon a table at one end of the schoolroom. Parents had been invited to come and join us in our celebrations. I had also written a brief note to the Vicar asking him to come and take our Harvest Festival service but I had no reply. We conducted our own very simple service, singing harvest hymns and thanking God for all the benefits of wind and rain and weather which had made our collection of gift so prolific. A group of parents took our gifts to a nearby hospital in Bridport. I was labelled as a trouble-maker, possibly a Communist, the worst possible label in the days when 'the red under bed' was the slogan used as a threat to peace and stability. In fact, I did not actively belong to any particular political party but I was concerned, as most teachers, for the well-being and moral, mental and physical growth of the children. Our school was not a hierarchy. Mrs Lennox, Auntie

85

Mary and later Mrs Rendell (dinner lady) and myself worked as a team each one essential for the harmonious working of the school. Democracy in action!

Another sports day

It was the summer term and, as the weeks passed, I knew that permission was required to hold the school sports on the extensive Vicarage lawn according to another of those age-old traditions. In company with Mrs Symes, one of the recently appointed Managers, I made the request at the end of morning service when the Vicar was available in person. One of the Churchwardens who was also a Manager was nearby and when I mentioned the school sports day he reminisced on past events when he, as a boy, had always won the high jump; but now it was skittles at which he was a winner!

Mrs Symes remembered a sudden thunderstorm which had sent everyone rushing into the Vicarage for shelter. I hastily intervened and said that if the weather was at all uncertain a restricted sports day would be held in the school.

Was it an act of God and the Vicar's prayers were answered or was I unduly prejudiced? (After all this account is written entirely from my own viewpoint of these events...) The weather left us in no doubt that sports day on a rain soaked Vicarage lawn was impossible.

Tables were stacked and chairs ranged around the room to accommodate parents and visitors. Makeshift races with balls, quoits, ropes, bowls, brooms and other random equipment were soon devised by Mrs Lennox and myself and, like the caucus race in 'Alice in Wonderland', everyone was applauded and everyone was a winner. Tea and buns for all left the schoolroom in a state of chaos but there were plenty of willing helpers and order was soon restored. The Vicar and his wife were invited but at the last minute a memo was received stating regrets and a previous engagement. No mention was ever made that his wife would be pleased to be associated with our activities either in the school or in other ways.

Personal

At the end of the summer term of 1958 I was informed by letter that a Managers' meeting would be held in the schoolroom during the first week of the summer holiday and I was invited to be present. There was no agenda so I thought that it would be a routine meeting. I had my report ready about the ongoing work of the school and a news item concerning my private life which I was hesitant to divulge.

The controversy over the use of the schoolroom as a village hall had never been completely resolved. While the good Canon was in office we had reached an amicable agreement and, when at all possible, meetings were held in the Reading Room. This was much smaller but was fully equipped for tea-making and card-playing and had the use of a large adjoining field for fair weather events. I was given to understand that it was much cheaper to use the school than the Reading Room! Two of the Managers who had been pupils during the pre-war years when 'schooling' was very limited, were very much in favour of holding dances in the school during holidays. The 'Village Hop' was very popular during the war years and had continued to be held until my arrival. I had compromised over the use of the school for events which could not be held in the limited space of the Reading Room but I had resisted every suggestion that the school be used as a dance hall. Times had changed and transport to social centres in nearby towns was easily available. As our schoolroom had become a busy workshop and centre of learning the question of dances to be held had never arisen.

But at the Managers' meeting held at the end of July 1958 I was told that dances would be held in the schoolroom at the discretion of the Managers and that this decision had the approval of all present. I had received no intimation that such a possibility had even been suggested. Obviously a previous meeting had been held – no doubt in the Vicarage – where it had been decided to inform me that such a decision had been taken. There was nothing I could do. The Managers were the custodians of the building and I was merely permitted to work there. I did not look at the newly appointed 'Mums' as I knew that support from them would have been over-ruled by the Vicar and the other four Managers, two of whom would have been indecisive but had thought it expedient to agree with the Vicar and his two supporters.

I had my own shock to deliver. I was pregnant I told them and added that my employers would be informed and that a supply teacher would be in charge during my enforced absence.

I do not remember the outcome of the meeting but no doubt we were all subdued and somewhat confused!

The realisation of my pregnancy during the previous May had come as a shock to myself. It is unbelievable that my husband and I were both so ignorant about methods of contraception. There had been abstinence for most of the time since Judith's birth due to fear and also from pressure of work both on the farm and subsequently from the change in our situation. Possibly I had become more relaxed now that the school was progressing so well and that Judith and Giles had been accepted. After the first shock my feelings about the pregnancy were mixed but I still remember lying in the bath feeling and watching the movements in this core of myself, experiencing the wonder of this new creation in my body; the wonder however tinged with apprehension. Would there be another chromosome defect or some other abnormality? I was 43 years old after all. Such uncertainties dissipated as the weeks passed; I knew that all would be well. I hugged the event to myself after a brief visit to the Doctor to confirm the pregnancy and to arrange for the birth to take place at home so that Judith and Giles would not have to be boarded out. (In the event, Giles spent the Christmas holidays with my brother's family in Clacton.) I did not tell my husband as he had make arrangements for a visit to his married sister in Scunthorpe where he was to be employed temporarily on the railway.

I thought that I could conceal my 'condition' until the autumn term when it would be necessary to inform the LEA in Dorchester of the situation.

It was a further shock when I was informed that I would take the mandatory six weeks leave before the birth and six weeks leave after the birth – three months *without* pay.

No doubt it was regrettable that I had not read the conditions for maternity leave as defined in my contract although, at the time of my appointment, the possibility of such a circumstance had never occurred to me! The news that I would receive no income, not even on the basis of being absent on sick leave, was indeed a shock as we were so dependent upon the income. The money from the farm sale had been invested by my husband in his name and I knew that I would have access to none of it.

The following correspondence highlights such conditions of employment for women which existed only forty years ago!

These are all copies of the originals which I have in my possession.

DORSET COUNTY COUNCIL
COUNTY HALL, DORCHESTER, DORSET

EDUCATION DEPARTMENT

JOHN HAYNES, M.A., COUNTY EDUCATION OFFICER

Telephone: Dorchester 1000

MY REF: AE/BG.EXT.311.   YOUR REF

16th September, 1958

Dear Madam,

Thank you for your letter dated the 12th September. I confirm that your maternity leave without salary will commence from the 29th September, and arrangements will be made for a relief teacher to attend at your school from this date.

Yours faithfully,

John Haynes

County Education Officer

Mrs. M. C. Ridout,
Whitechurch Canonicorum School,
Nr. Bridport,
Dorset

EDUCATION DEPARTMENT

JOHN HAYNES, M.A., COUNTY EDUCATION OFFICER

Telephone: Dorchester 1000 Ext. 311.

MY REF: JG/CN.   YOUR REF

22nd September, 1958

Dear Mrs Ridout,

Thank you for your letter of the 17th September, 1958, addressed to Mr. Galley. I am very sorry that you did not fully understand the terms of the leave of absence regulations as regards maternity leave. These regulations are referred to in the Standard Conditions of Tenure and are explained on Page 26 of the Committee's Handbook. The minimum period of maternity leave is six weeks before and six weeks after confinement. I regret that the normal sick leave regulations do not apply in these circumstances. Will you please let me know when you will be commencing your maternity leave.

I am sorry that my reply cannot be helpful as no provision is made for the payment of salary during maternity leave.

Yours sincerely,

John Haynes

Mrs. M. C. Ridout,
Whitechurch Canonicorum School,
Nr. Bridport,
Dorset

MY REF: WE/CN.   YOUR REF

30th September, 1958

Dear Mrs. Ridout,

Thank you for your letter. I am sorry to find that so much difficulty surrounds your maternity leave and that your financial circumstances are so awkward as to encourage you in feminist and suffragette tendencies. I hope that you won't get round to chaining yourself to the railings at Whitechurch school.

But don't blame the male members of the Committee or Department. The maternity leave regulation was thought up nationally not to make life difficult for you but to make it possible for a woman teacher not only to have a family but to hang on to her job or career too, if she wished to or was compelled to do so. I cannot however lighten the burden for you since the financial effect of these regulations is administered by the County Treasurer. This means a twelve weeks minimum loss of salary and I feel sure in any case that your doctor would agree with the medical authorities that six weeks before and after is very much in the interests of your health.

Yours sincerely,
W. Easton
County Education Officer

Mrs. M. C. Ridout,
Whitechurch Canonicorum School,
Nr. Bridport,
Dorset

National Union of Teachers
Benevolent & Orphan Fund Teacher Provident Society
Teachers Assurance Co. Ltd Schoolmaster & Woman Teachers Chronicle
TELEPHONE   HAMILTON HOUSE
EUSTON 2442-7   MABLEDON PLACE
TELEGRAMS   L O N D O N W C 1
CURRICULUM KINCROSS LONDON
GENERAL SECRETARY SIR RONALD GOULD MA HON. FEIS

MOMM/BW.O

6th October, 1958

Dear Mrs. Ridout,

In reply to your letter of October 2nd I can inform you that a number of counties do make payment to married women teachers during the three months compulsory maternity leave. The pattern varies over the country some counties paying salary during this leave of absence as if it were normal sick pay without affecting the entitlement, others will make payments which vary considerably from county to county, for example, one Authority will pay six weeks full pay before the birth and twelve weeks half pay after the birth, another will pay three months full before the birth and three months half after. Another Authority pays one month full before birth and nothing after. In every case payment is subject to National Insurance deductions and in many cases an undertaking to return to the service is required. In some cases pay is withheld until resumption of duty.

The Union is at present making a full scale investigation of this overall picture with a view to seeking some form of National Agreement. I am afraid it will be quite impossible at this stage to comply with your request to tell you which counties do pay as it would be a very incomplete picture, but if you are seeking information about any particular counties with a view of seeking employment there I shall be happy to make enquiries for your.

Yours sincerely,
Gwen Morris

Mrs. M. C. Ridout,
The School House
Whitechurch Canonicorum School,
Nr. Bridport,
Dorset

Oct. 8th 1958

Dear Mr Easton,

I don't want to prolong this correspondence unnecessarily, and
for the mere sake of airing my views; but I feel very strongly
about this business of being cut off without a shilling simply
because one's sex is that of a child-bearing female. I thought that
my surprise at receiving nothing at all for the three months was
not completely unfounded, so I wrote to Hamilton House for
further information, and enclosed is an excerpt from the reply
which does indeed justify my attitude. This maternity leave
regulation is by no means a national jurisdiction (as in fact it
should be) but is a purely local arrangement in which the Dorset
authority seems to behave in an extremely mercenary manner. It
certainly does nothing to ease the business of having a child, but
merely adds a burden of financial worry to the female who
should be stupid or unlucky enough to add to the responsibility
of motherhood to those already involved by her career.

That the Dorset LEA sees fit to employ married women at
all – and so presumably places some sort of value on the work
they do – should surely justify an act to support them during
such emergencies. If sick benefit can be, and is, paid to both
sexes for recognised periods of time, regardless of personal
conditions or the nature of the illness, why should married
women be penalised for a condition of health which surely
should be encouraged rather than condemned in the so-called
educated section of the community. Presumably one is to be
grateful that the job is still available after twelve weeks of
enforced absence, and yet there are many teachers of both sexes
who are absent for very much longer periods and who never
need to entertain the slightest doubt about the security of their
jobs.

I cannot help feeling that a lot of young married women in

the county who would like to have children will be severely prejudiced when they realise the financial loss they will have to face. A healthy confinement is perhaps not such a disaster, but it often happens that the woman is not in a condition to work for much longer than the three months, and if she is to face this without any financial help she will either avoid such a condition with all the means at her command, or she will remove to a county where conditions are more considerate to the married woman who has to face the possibility of having children.

I am not grinding a personal axe, as I have made my arrangements and have come to terms with the situation; and I'm not directing this to you personally, as you have always been most helpful and considerate in every way; but there is no-one else on the LEA to whom I can appeal. I often think that it is a pity that there is no female representative on the executive staff to deal with the many problems peculiar to women and which can affect their jobs; problems which many young women would find it difficult to talk over with a man. In the 1930s there was a certain famous – or infamous to some – Ellen Miller on the staff; and I have personal reason to know how invaluable was her help to the young women teachers in connection with their work, and in their personal difficulties. (Which had a good deal of effect upon their jobs.) Now there is no-one except yourself and Mr. Haynes to whom I have also written in similar vein, as I feel that this non-payment for maternity leave is a question of policy which should be examined.

I am sorry to be another fly in the ointment – no doubt I would be better employed in knitting little woollies!

Yours sincerely,

M. C. Ridout

School House
Whitechurch Canonicorum
Nr. Bridport, Dorset

Oct. 8th. 1958

Dear Mr. Haynes,

I have been indulging in rather a lengthy correspondence with Mr. Easton on a situation which has just arisen in my own life but which I am sure must be pertinent to many of your married women employees. I am due to have a baby at the end of December, and have been informed that the compulsory leave of three months is to be without any salary or sick benefit whatsoever. This came as rather a shock especially at a time when expenses are greater than at normal times. Regardless of my own personal condition I feel that this could, and probably does, cause great hardship. Most married women in my experience are teaching because circumstances force them to do so and, in the majority of cases, their income is the staple support of the family. To face a period of three months – possibly even longer – without any financial security from their employers for an event for which they are entirely at the mercy of their sex struck me as being very unfair.

That the Dorset LEA sees fit to employ married women at all – and so, presumably, place some sort of value on the work they do – surely should justify an act to help support them during such emergencies. If sick benefit can be, and is, paid to both sexes for recognised periods of times, regardless of personal conditions or the nature of the illness, why should married women be penalised for a condition of health which surely should be encouraged rather than condemned in the so-called educated section of the community? Presumably one is to be grateful that the job is still available after twelve weeks of enforced absence; and yet there are many teachers of both sexes who are absent for many much longer periods and who never need to entertain the slightest doubt about the security of their jobs.

What makes the situation seem even more unfair is that conditions vary according to the county – (please see excerpt quoted from information supplied by the NUT) and that Dorset LEA has exploited the situation in the most mercenary way. I cannot help feeling that a lot of young married women in the county who would like to have children will be severely prejudiced when they realise the financial loss they will have to face. a healthy confinement is perhaps not such a disaster but it often happens that the woman is not in a condition for work for a longer period than the three months and, if she is to face this without any financial help, she will either avoid such a condition with the all the means at her command, or she will remove to a county where conditions are more considerate to the married woman who faces the possibility of having children. I should think that either action is to be deplored.

I am making this protest to you as well as to Mr. Easton as I feel that attention should be drawn to this policy which must have such adverse repercussions on the lives of a reasonably large section of your teaching staff.

Yours sincerely,

M. C. Ridout

(Mr. Haynes was the Chief Education Officer at the time. Mr. Easton was the deputy Education Officer responsible for Primary Schools.)

DORSET COUNTY COUNCIL
COUNTY HALL, DORCHESTER, DORSET

EDUCATION DEPARTMENT

JOHN HAYNES, M.A., COUNTY EDUCATION OFFICER

Telephone: Dorchester 1000 Ext. 311.

MY REF: JG/CN.   OUR REF

10th October, 1958

Dear Mrs. Ridout,

Thank you for your letter of 8th October. I also acknowledge the one which you have sent to Mr. Easton because he is at present away from the office.

I think that an answer to your complaints rests on two foundations. The first is that when you were appointed to the headship of Whitechurch Canonicorum School you entered into a contract with the Education Committee by accepting the conditions of tenure which were sent to you. Those conditions included one about maternity leave which specified the period of leave which must be taken and said that it would be without salary. In one of your earlier letters to Mr. Easton you said that you are not the type of person who willingly resorts to wading through the applicable information until pushed. That attitude cannot be the responsibility of the Education Committee and it surely is a matter of prudence to study the terms of any agreement before entering into it. If one does not one is not on firm ground to complain afterwards.

The second foundation of the reply is a general one. You talk about married women being penalised for a condition of health. I think that you are really objecting, not to the policy of the County Education Committee but to the established order of creation. Arrangement for sick pay take account of accidents or illness which are no-one's personal responsibility; pregnancy is obviously something different and employers are quite entitled to feel that absence from duty because of confinement is

98

different in its nature from absence because of a broken limb. I think that you will find that very large number of insurance schemes specifically exclude pregnancy from any benefits and one can conclude from this that there is a fair body of establish opinion on the subject. You ought also to gear in mind that, as you say in your letter, you have security of employment, which is surely a big consideration.

Yours sincerely

John Haynes

County Education Officer

Mrs. M. C. Ridout,
Whitechurch Canonicorum School,
Nr. Bridport,
Dorset

National Union of Teachers
Benevolent & Orphan Fund Teacher Provident Society
Teachers Assurance Co. Ltd Schoolmaster & Woman Teachers Chronicle
TELEPHONE   HAMILTON HOUSE
EUSTON 2442-7   MABLEDON PLACE
TELEGRAMS   L O N D O N W C 1
CURRICULUM KINCROSS LONDON
GENERAL SECRETARY SIR RONALD GOULD MA HON. FEIS

MOMM/BW.O

6th October, 1958

Dear Mrs. Ridout,

I was sorry when I received your letter to learn the unfortunate circumstances which accompany what should be for you a very happy event. Dorset I am aware is an Authority which is amongst the least helpful in respect of Maternity Leave, but I will send your letter on to Mr. Tann, our Regional Official, to see if he can make it convenient to visit you at an early date. It is possible that, when he is armed with the facts of your case, he may be able to secure the sympathy of your Authority to treat your case exceptionally in view of the fact that you are the bread-winner for your family, but please do not build too much hope in this respect. It is indeed unfortunate that you have elected not to pay in National Health Contributions. We have frequently advised our married women members both through the columns of the Schoolmaster and through special National Insurance leaflets giving them entitlement to sickness benefit, unemployment benefit and Maternity allowance, but this will I am afraid be of small comfort to you at this time. I only mention it so you may know we have not failed in our duty to advise married women teachers in this respect. I am grateful to you that you are public spirited enough to send me the particulars of your case in the hope that they will be of help to us in the investigation that we are making. I am sure your case will make a valuable contribution to our argument when we seek to protect others of our women colleagues from similar circumstances by our negotiations with the Authorities to secure a National Agreement.

I am glad you found it reassuring to read 'Woman Official'

under my signature. I only wish that I could do more for you in the present circumstances.

Yours sincerely

Gwen Morris

Woman Official

School House,
Whitechurch Canonicorum,
Nr. Bridport, Dorset.

13th. October.

Dear Mr. Haynes,

I am quite aware that I must aide by the terms of agreement contracted at the commencement of my employment with Dorset LEA; and having registered my protest there is no more to be done.

But I just cannot accept passively your statement that I am objecting to the established order of creation. Nothing could be further from my whole religious and logical (I hope) outlook on life. My objection is to the attitude that this particular county chooses to adopt towards conditions caused by the established natural order; and especially in comparison with the attitude of other counties to this particular situation.

I realise, of course, the alternative!

Yours sincerely

Margaret C. Ridout.

M. C. Ridout

I was in school for part of each day during the weeks of my enforced leave of absence during the latter half of the autumn term. I needed to oversee and to be in contact with the work programmes I had initiated. The supply teacher was very tolerant about my intrusions and welcomed my supplies of coffee and tea as we talked over the ongoing work of the pupils.

It was not so easy to be so involved during the enforced weeks of retirement after the birth. Mother and child had to get used to each other. A routine had to be established so that a return to work would be possible. 'Auntie' Jane and 'Auntie' Mary were two great allies and I was often reminded of the elephant who has an attendant 'auntie' after the birth of her offspring! Between us all we managed; Helen is alive and well at the age of 41 years and with a child of her own. Judith and Giles also have survived those difficult years!

Public and Private Lives

It was difficult to disassociate one's private life from public observance of the school with myself as the head teacher. Every aspect of a teacher's life was under constant scrutiny and even more so in a village situation. Many teachers in such schools chose to live at a distance from their place of work and with wider ownership of cars this became more possible. School houses were often used to accommodate the school caretaker. I had not been too concerned about this interest in my private affairs as, idealistically, I believed that the school (myself and family included) should be a centre for the village and that the school should be an extension of my own family and my family an extension of the school.

I was forced to rethink my role in terms of a more professional commitment when two pupils, who previously had been transferred from the small private school, were withdrawn from our own school. The father came to see me one day after school about his daughters' work. I was pushing the baby in her pram back from Auntie Mary's and asked him to come and join me for a cup of tea – all very informal and 'motherly'... I do not think that he made any complaints and I was surprised when later I was informed that the girls would attend a Convent school in Lyme Regis.

The number of pupils in the school had more than doubled since I had been in charge and this reversal forced me to consider a situation about which I had become complacent. The father and his wife were sensible and intelligent parents and if they had doubts about my suitability as a teacher for their daughters it was possible that others might think the same. I needed to assess more objectively the duality of my role and to see it from the viewpoint of the father and other parents. However competent I might be in the classroom the facts were that I had an ailing husband who was often away and three children, one a baby and another mentally handicapped. Confidence in my ability to cope inevitably must be shaken. I decided that my earlier ideal of school/family working in tandem would have to be modified. I should have made an appointment to see the father after school but on a more official basis in my role as head teacher and without the obvious sign of my domestic life. I must begin to separate the two roles. I began to think in terms of moving out of the school house and away from the immediate vicinity of the village; but there were so many practical difficulties. I needed the support of the two 'aunties' and, in the evenings, it was easier for me to go through the adjoining door into the schoolroom to organise the school work.

There were other problems concerning my husband and myself. He was not a fit person and had been unable to keep the jobs he had taken in the locality; neither was he able to fill the contemporary concept of being a house-husband. Eventually it was decided that he would buy a house elsewhere and that the children and I would join him at weekends and for holidays. A suitable house was found in Uplyme on the outskirts of Lyme Regis and he moved in. My curious neighbour who lived in the pub opposite to the school watched every move as we loaded a bed, a table and a few other necessities which could be spared into a borrowed van. I explained briefly that living conditions in the school house were extremely cramped with the addition of the baby, that my husband had been offered work as a gardener in Lyme Regis and that we would use 'Croggs' (the name of the house) as a family home for holidays and occasional weekends.

In fact the separation was more permanent than we realised at the time.

I had hoped that 'Croggs' would have provided a retreat for all of us but it was not to be. No provision was made by my husband to accommodate a visiting family and he retreated back into the comfort of his bachelor days seeing the children only when I took them for brief visits.

It became even more necessary to find a 'retreat' when dissension over the use of the schoolroom escalated into open confrontation. I could not afford to take the children away for holidays. We went camping near Sidmouth in the summer but

105

we had no proper equipment and with the addition of a baby it was all too difficult.

A chink in the clouds came in the form of a £40,00 tax rebate and during the Easter break of 1960 I spent it on a holiday in the island of Sark. We stayed in a rented cottage, the weather was kind and it was an idyllic respite from all the controversies, the antagonisms and anxieties of living in the school house – at that time. The tax rebate had come as a result of yet another financial dispute. Tax payable was deducted from my salary at source and was based on the joint incomes of my husband and myself. Eventually I discovered that a previous rebate had been made to my husband! After further correspondence with the tax office I was able to get a separate assessment and my tax level was reduced considerably. I also received the £40.00 rebate – a gift from the gods!

My health had become affected. I suffered from migraines and then had a partial collapse. My mother – not young herself – Auntie Mary and Auntie Jane came to the rescue. The baker who delivered our bread and whose son was in the school lent me a tent. I was given a week's sick leave and our well-known supply teacher took charge again in the school. I drove the old Morris 8 to Branscombe and pitched the tent on a stretch of wasteland (now a car park).

I remember that it rained incessantly. I walked and walked along the foreshore and along the cliff pathways which thread their hidden ways through the undergrowth of the cliffs between Branscombe and Sidmouth. It was there that I saw the occasional hut, or chalet, tucked away behind shrubs and stunted trees. And I met with 'Gozzie' (Mr Gosling) and his donkey. He was elderly – or so it seemed – and grew crops of early potatoes and spring flowers in his 'plats' – or plots – which he had cleared from the vegetation and had cultivated over the years. He took his produce on the donkey to sell in Sidmouth market. He told me that he kept the pathways open and I understood that he was the unofficial warden, or guardian of the cliffs. (The whole area has been under the control of National Heritage for many years since then.)

I asked about the few chalets I had seen; they all seemed to be deserted. They were just used for holidays, he said, and he kept an eye on them but few people ever came that way. The paths were steep and in wet weather they were slippery and difficult to negotiate due to streams which crossed them at intervals. I also thought of the places I had passed where the vegetation had fallen away and there were sheer drops to the beach below. I asked if any of the chalets were available to be let or to be sold. He didn't think so and the cliff top was owned by the local farmer who did not encourage visitors.

I sat in the shelter of an overhanging hedge and looked out to sea. The rain had lifted and the view of sea and cliffs stretched westwards as far as Start Point near Torquay. Below was a small sheltered bay, the water clear with patches of seaweed and rocks.

I walked those paths for two days, pursued Mr Gosling until eventually he said that there was a hut which was almost completely overgrown. It had been erected by a middle-aged couple years ago but when the husband died he had seen no-one come to stay there. He took me to see it down a narrow stony pathway to a corner hidden by bushes through which part of a felted roof was just visible. Mr Gosling cut a way through and on a rocky platform set into the cliff was the chalet. It was about 20ft. long and 10ft. wide and there was a lean-to which had been used as a kitchen said my guide. It was indeed derelict and in need of minor repairs and paint; nothing that Giles and I could not do! After more persuasion Gozzie said that he had the address of the owner at home. I called for it on my way back to the school. I wrote hopefully and for a modest sum which I could just afford the chalet was mine.

It was a perfect retreat and less than 30 miles from Whitechurch. The chalet was unapproachable except on foot although in dry weather a car could be driven to the cliff top – with permission from the farmer. For any curious or unwanted visitors I always mentioned that it was a perfect habitat for adders!

We picnicked and camped in comfort while we cleared the small site and had a bonfire of the decayed and mildewed furnishings. By degrees we carried metal framed beds, foam mattresses and sleeping bags, a table and a small chest of drawers down to the chalet. Eventually Judith and Helen were fitted with small back-packs in which they carried their share of food and small items for the 'holiday'. Judith used to put up a resistance on reaching the cliff edge where there was a small drop on to the narrow path but Helen was always able to persuade and encourage her to make the effort when I usually failed! Gozzie, as we now called him, was most helpful and brought us a paraffin cooker which had been discarded from one of the other chalets. Light was provided by candles and a paraffin hurricane lantern. There was water pumped by a 'ram' in a nearby small clearing but I was soon to provide our own supply by inserting a small tank at the head of a stream further up the cliff. Plastic piping from an outlet drilled in the base of the tank snaked down through the undergrowth to the chalet. With a bracket attached to the wall and a tap affixed to the end of the piping we had our own water supply, clean and fresh and which never dried up even through the hot dry weeks of August.

The place was a suntrap, warm whenever there was sun, even in winter. Two sturdy fir trees were rooted just below the flat rock on which the chalet stood and from there it was possible to view the whole stretch of the beach below and to see the occasional seal. We swam – Giles and I enjoyed snorkelling – we picnicked, explored and relaxed in that delightful retreat; even the cat began to accept is as home. Only the very closest friends were invited to visit. The steep pathways and the adders were deterrents for all but those who shared out enthusiasms. For the next five years we enjoyed the seclusion of our second home on the cliffs of Branscombe.

Finances

I had initiated a school fund soon after my arrival in the village. I knew that the capitation allowance would not be sufficient to provide the equipment and extra books which I considered to be necessary. Whist drives had proved to be popular and lucrative and caused little disruption to the ongoing work of the children. Jumble sales, school concerts – with 'For Sale' tables – also made useful contributions to the fund for which one of the Managers was made responsible.

I remember that a tape recorder was one of our first acquisitions. We joined a record club and used my daughter's record player to play light classical music while we ate our mid-day dinners brought in containers from Lyme Regis. We also belonged to an Art club which loaned out large framed prints on a termly exchange basis. We gave to charity. Father Borelli and his work with the urchins in Naples was one of our favourites. Father Borelli paid a brief visit to Bridport and inspired all who heard him talk about his work with the 'uffici'.

I knew that money was needed for repairs to the school building for which the church was responsible but I had always stipulated that money raised by the parents should be used only for the children and their education. Much later when I became aware of the amount being spent on refurbishing the Church I expected that money would be made available for the more essential repairs to the school. However, I was to be mistaken.

The letting of the schoolroom to such groups as the Young Farmers, the W I, the Amateur Dramatic Society and so forth had provided a small income used towards the cost of minor repairs and also provided for an annual payment of £20.00 to an insurance scheme which was supposed to cover any emergency with regards to the maintenance of the building. Money raised from the lettings and the use of it had not been my concern and I assumed that the recordings of such transactions were included with the Church's financial affairs. Later, when relationships between Church and School became strained over the problem of financial resources I enquired about the money raised from the lettings but I was told that no separate fund existed.

Confrontation

Discussions between myself and the Managers were in abeyance during my enforced absence. One of the ladies who recently had come to live in the village took over the Church choir. She had a trained voice and was soon joined by others with musical connections. They were soon to be robed with ruffs and head 'caps' and I withdrew to sit with the congregation. Christmas for me that year was spent quietly at home awaiting the imminent birth. Giles spent the holiday with my brother's family and my husband was away in Scunthorpe. I gave no further thought to the possibility of holding dances in the schoolroom; for the next weeks I was fully occupied with my own affairs.

I was given notice soon after my return to work that a dance would be held in the school during the Easter break. There was nothing I could do about it and it seemed that there was no one to whom I could appeal. I could not go away; the baby was barely three months old and I was extremely short of money. The chalet on the cliffs was not to materialise for another two years. I knew that I had no alternative but to accept the situation.

I cleared the schoolroom as far as possible, stacked books in piles on the shelves and almost wished that I had not dispensed with those old worm-eaten cupboards. I decided that I would attend the dance for a short time in an effort to co-operate rather than to renew my objections.

It was a pleasant enough evening with a local band and the room full of noisy and heavy-footed dancers most of whom were unknown to me. Two of the Managers were in charge and the Vicar put in a brief appearance during the evening. There was only one incident which I recall. A young man unknown to me picked up one of the books from the shelves and made some derogatory comment about it to me; obviously he knew who I was. I decided to ignore him and to return to the house. I had kept the door through to the kitchen bolted on the inside and returned through the playground where there was more to offend my sense of propriety! The village hall had been the scene for many a quick 'affair' no doubt but, to me, this was a school and the whole event was an affront to me as the head teacher and to those who shared in our beliefs and values.

There were to be other dances but, as they were held in the school holidays, I often managed to be away. Eventually the chalet on the Branscombe cliffs provided the perfect retreat and we spent all our holidays there, even Christmas! so that I was able to ignore the mis-use of our schoolroom. However, as time passed, the building itself gave cause for concern. The floor was showing signs of wear and after an inspection by the County Architect, it was stated that the floor joists were rotten and that soon the whole floor would have to be renewed. I still was not reconciled to the school/village hall situation and eventually I wrote to Canon Maples, the Secretary of Salisbury Diocesan Council of Education, for further advice.

The following correspondence which I have retained over the years highlights a situation which was not at all uncommon in such villages at that time. Small wonder that so many of our village schools have been closed and removed from local autonomy.

The school in Whitechurch became Voluntarily Controlled so that the building itself was the responsibility of the local Education Authority in Dorchester; but the threat of possible closure was only to be delayed. There were plans for an Area School to be sited in Charmouth which would incorporate the schools of Whitechurch Canonicorum and Wootton Fitzpaine.

1971

The village school in Whitechurch Canonicorum was closed.

The pupils were transferred to Charmouth School and merged into classes of 36, 36, 40 and 28. (The numbers are taken from the school log book in Charmouth.)

School House,
Whitechurch Canonicorum
Nr. Bridport, Dorset.

Feb. 23rd. 1961.

Dear Canon Maples,

For the past five years there has been some controversy between the Managers and myself about the advisability of holding public dances in the schoolroom. This does not imply that there is any unpleasant relationship between us, but it is a point over which I feel that a more disinterested opinion would be of some service – certainly to myself.

Two years ago, while I happened to be away for a week, the Managers met and decided that, despite my objections which I had expressed at a previous meeting, public dances should be held during the school holidays at the discretion of the Managers, and I was told that the decision had been unanimous, although privately four of the Managers told me that they sympathised with my situation. Since then, it is true that there have been very few dances, mainly because I know that my disapproval holds their frequency in some sort of check. I accepted the decision of course, but whenever a dance is arranged I cannot help feeling that it is not right. I know that I may be wrong, and this is where I hope that your unbiased opinion will help. I must list my objections below, but as the school mistress here it is inevitable that I am prejudiced. To me the building is essentially a school – a centre for cultural and semi-cultural activities, and as a village meeting place, to none of which activities have I ever raised the slightest objection. It is only the question of *public* dances which are attended by people from many other places, to whom the school is just another hall towards which they feel no responsibility.

And here firstly I feel very conscious, and perhaps un-necessarily responsible for the state of the building itself. When I came here in September 1955, the building was a shell which

112

had been used primarily as a village hall. The Education Authority spent a considerable sum of money upon redecorating the whole of the interior, renewing the playground, and upon new equipment to which we ourselves have added considerably through the Children's Fund. The Managers themselves (only one of whom still remains in office) under the chairmanship of Canon Davidson, undertook to provide modern sanitation and alterations to the teacher's house. Our own village people know this and treat the school with due care; but it bothers me when I see the odd cigarette burn on a desk or shelf or the odd bracket broken down in a cloakroom. Now *nothing* at all serious has been done, but I always feel that it's a possibility. I am also worried about possibilities of fire, especially as there are no fire-fighting appliances on the premises.

Secondly there is the state of the floor. This is in an extremely bad condition. The county architect had it examined and found that there is extensive dry rot in the joists so that one day the whole floor will have to be renewed. The delay is due to finance, and this being an aided school, naturally we are far down on the list. The Managers have been informed that the floor quite definitely is unfit for the public dances.

Thirdly, when there is to be a dance, I have to make sure that all books and apparatus are stacked away, and even in holidays this is very inconvenient, as a good deal of my preparation and checking work has to be done then. For instance, there is to be a dance in the Easter holiday, the holiday in which I do all the stock-taking, and the ordering of books and equipment for the following year. I cannot do this with everything packed away, and it's a job I cannot do in two or three days. I have a family of three children to look after, and I have to fit my extra-schoolwork around them. During the summer holidays I make out all my schemes of work for each group for the entire year, check the past year's work and so forth. Again this cannot be done without the books.

I also object – pretty strongly on this point – on the unsuitable sanitary arrangements. The boys' urinal and two lavatories are at one end of the playground away from the main building, and there is no electric light fitted in them. Obviously on a dark night strangers do not know where the lavatories are, with the result that the playgrounds are used instead. Not only do I find it very offensive – it occurs even under my bedroom window – but I think it's dangerous from a health viewpoint. I was perhaps rather vehement on this point and last time a lantern was hung in the lavatories – but still the playgrounds were used.

***

Finally I object to the dances from my own personal angle. You may or may not know that the house is directly adjacent to the schoolroom. In fact my kitchen opens directly into it. It's true that for me dance band music is anathema – but if I was the only one concerned I could arrange to be out. It so happens that I have three young children aged 11, 9 and 2 and half years so that it isn't possible to stay out until 12 or 1 am – even if I so wished. The noise, of course, is impossible to ignore, the dividing wall has no thickness, and it's quite impossible for anyone to sleep until it's all over. Quite frankly, when I came here I didn't reckon on having to live next door to a dance-hall, however infrequent the dances. I cannot imagine that any of the Managers would willingly tolerate such a situation for their own families.

I felt at first that I was being something of a kill-joy, and certainly I have no objections to dancing. Unfortunately there is no village hall here, and for years and years before my arrival dances were held here pretty often, to the detriment of the school. I have asked some of the younger generation about these dances and they freely admit that dances in the surrounding towns are better; and in these days when every family has a motor car I do not feel that I am being unduly hard on the youngsters if I deprive them of the few odd dances here.

Two years ago I saw Mr Easton on the subject to find out the official attitude, and he told me that they were one hundred per cent behind me, but that officially they could do nothing as the building technically is under the control of the Managers. I do not feel that I can again appeal to him. So I finally decided to put the case to you as fairly as I am able; and I shall more readily agree to what I feel must be the unbiased opinion of someone who probably has much experience in problems of this kind.

I have informed the Managers that I intend to refer the matter to a higher authority – for the sake of my successors as much as for myself. There has been no response to my note to them – so now I feel that this letter must be sent.

Yours sincerely

M. C. Ridout

Salisbury Diocesan Council of Education
Founded 1839 Constituted the Statutory Diocesan Education Authority under the
Diocesan Education Committees Measure 1943. Incorporated 1949.
CHAIRMAN: THE RIGHT REV. THE LORD BISHOP OF SALISBURY

The Rev Canon Jeffrey S Maples MA   CHURCH HOUSE
Secretary and Director of Religious Education CRANE STREET
Group Capt. R W Collinson (Retd.) CA   SALISBURY
Telephone 2675
JSM/EH

Dear Mrs. Ridout,

I am sorry you had to write again about this vexed question of holding public dances in your school. Actually since you first wrote I have had an opportunity of discussing it with Mr. Easton, and find that we both agree that they are undesirable.

I find that I also wrote to the Rev. G.V. Syer on the 11th September 1958 on this subject as follows:

'In general I should think it undesirable to hold dances in term time as the contents of the school would be disarranged and there would be a possibility of damage. There would seem to be less objection to a dance in the holidays where the school is a detached building. I remember, however, from my last visit, that the teacher's house and the school are very closely bound up together and I should have thought it undesirable that there should be public activities in the school which would be disturbing to the teacher as a private resident. I should think that the Managers would probably all agree that they would not want a public village dance, probably continuing until midnight, on their own premises and would wish to extend the same consideration to the head mistress, especially as I believe she has young children. There does not seem to be the same objection to quieter functions such as whist drives, which are probably equally lucrative.'

I also offered to meet the Managers, but this offer has not been taken up.

I enclose a copy of a further letter to the Vicar. Incidentally I am wondering whether a licence might be needed for a public dance in which case objections could be lodged in the Magistrate's Court to such a licence being granted. If the practice continues, I suggest it might be worth your while to consult the Clerk to the local Magistrates, or if you preferred, to get Mr. Tann of the NUT to handle this for you.

I am sorry you should have this trouble.

Yours sincerely,

Jeffrey S Maples

Mrs M. C. Ridout,
The School House,
Whitechurch Canonicorum,
Bridport, Dorset.

Salisbury Diocesan Council of Education
Founded 1839 Constituted the Statutory Diocesan Education Authority under the
Diocesan Education Committees Measure 1943. Incorporated 1949.
CHAIRMAN: THE RIGHT REV. THE LORD BISHOP OF SALISBURY

The Rev Canon Jeffrey S Maples MA   CHURCH HOUSE
Secretary and Director of Religious Education   CRANE STREET
Group Capt. R W Collinson (Retd.) CA   SALISBURY
Telephone 2675
JSM/EH

24th March, 1961

C O P Y

Dear Mr. Syer,

You will remember consulting me in 1958 about dances at Whitechurch Canonicorum School. In my reply I said:

'In general I should think it undesirable to hold dances in term time as the contents of the school would be disarranged and there would be a possibility of damage. There would seem to be less objection to a dance in the holidays where the school is a detached building. I remember, however, from my last visit, that the teacher's house and the school are very closely bound up together and I should have thought it undesirable that there should be public activities in the school which would be disturbing to the teacher as a private resident. I should think that the Managers would probably all agree that they would not want a public village dance, probably continuing until midnight, on their own premises and would wish to extend the same consideration to the head mistress, especially as I believe she had young children. There does not seem to be the same objection to quieter functions such as whist drives, which are probably equally lucrative.'

I understand that public dances are still held from time to time, and should think that they must be a considerable disturbance to the head mistress and her young family living next door. I also understand there are no fire-fighting appliances and that there is extensive dry rot in the joists of the floor; and that the playground is liable to be fouled during and after a

118

dance.

There do seem to be very strong grounds for the Managers to decide that they could not allow the school to be used for this purpose any longer, and I am sure this Council would support any such decision. I understand that the local Education Authority would also support it.

I have no doubt that the Managers would wish to do the best thing for the school, the village and the headmistress, but they may be under some pressure in the village. It occurs to me that a public dance may possibly need a licence, and if so, that the granting of such a licence could be opposed. If there are reasons which prevent the Managers taking a firm stand in this matter, it might be possible that opposition to a licence could be entered by the Education Authority or this council, or the NUT. One would hope that this should not be necessary.

I should be grateful if you would let me know whether the facts are as I understand them.

Yours sincerely

Jeffrey S Maples

The Rev. G.V. Syer,
The Vicarage,
Whitechurch Canonicorum,
Bridport, Dorset.

30.3.61

Dear Mrs Ridout,

At the Managers meeting held yesterday I was requested to take certain action, but you will appreciate that I can not do anything until after Easter. Later I shall be writing to you.

I return your papers – I picked them up with mine and put them all in the file together.

Yours sincerely,

G V Syer

DORSET EDUCATION COMMITTEE

========================

Whitechurch Canonicorum School,
Nr. Bridport, Dorset.

April 5th. 1961

Dear Canon Maples,

Thank you very much indeed for your letter and for all the information concerning your attitude to the dances in this school. But I'm afraid that the Vicar is annoyed at the stand I am taking over this matter.

There was a Manager's meeting held a week ago at which I requested that all the correspondence should be put before them. I left all my correspondence for them to see. I have received no information of any conclusions reached – Mr. Syer merely wrote me a note to say that he had been requested to take certain action. I am wondering if he has asked you to come and see the Managers – as you once suggested. If so I would like to say that I am going away for the whole of next week, and that if there is a meeting, I would like to be present, as the issue so closely concerns me.

Thanking you again for your support.

Yours sincerely
M. C. Ridout

DORSET EDUCATION COMMITTEE

========================

Whitechurch Canonicorum School,
Nr. Bridport, Dorset.

April 5th. 1961

Dear Mr. Easton,

I am having some difficulty about this business of dances in the school and I'm finding it increasingly difficult to work with this new Vicar. Canon Maples wrote and quite strongly emphasised that it is not suitable to hold public dances here. I passed this correspondence on to the Vicar – and a week ago a Managers' meeting was called, presumably to discuss this opinion. I have been informed of nothing of the outcome of the meeting except to receive a note from the Vicar stating that he had been asked to take a certain action. He knows that I shall be away on holiday all next week, I think it is quite possible to ask you and Canon Maples to come and see the Managers in my absence. I have written to Canon Maples to ask that no such meeting be held without my presence – and I would be very grateful to you if you would do nothing until I have seen you about it all.

I'm very sorry to have to bother you about this – but could you please spare me a half an hour on either Mon. or Tues. of April 17th., 18th.?

Yours sincerely

M. C. Ridout

THE VICARAGE,
WHITECHURCH CANONICORUM
BRIDPORT, DORSET.

Resolution passed at the Meeting held on Monday. May 15th. Of the School Managers with Mr. Easton and Canon Maples.

'That Mr. Easton's offer to talk to Mrs. Ridout about the proper relationship which should exist between the Headmistress and the Managers be accepted, and that if Mrs. Ridout agrees to take steps to raise £20 per annum towards the Managers funds, then the Managers agree to withhold their right, to hold dances in the school for the time being at least.'

TEL: CHIDEOCK 223   THE VICARAGE,
                              WHITECHURCH CANONICORUM
                                  BRIDPORT, DORSET.

May 18th 1961

Dear Mrs. Ridout

I enclose a copy of the resolution passed at the meeting on Monday.

The £20 was really based on the VSA £18 which I believe you once agreed to raise through your Fund.

Yours sincerely

G V Syer

DORSET COUNTY COUNCIL
COUNTY HALL, DORCHESTER, DORSET

EDUCATION DEPARTMENT

J.R. BRADSHAW, M.A., COUNTY EDUCATION OFFICER

Telephone: Dorchester 1000

YOUR REF:
MY REF: WE/CN.

24th May, 1961

PERSONAL

Dear Mrs. Ridout,

Thank you for your letter dated 18th May enclosing the Vicar's 'ultimatum'.

This reply is entirely personal and not for use or quotation. Not only did I have your letter on Friday morning but I had a visit in person from Mr. Syer who produced your letter to him and is obviously perturbed about the whole situation just as your are and as I am. One of the troubles about the Aids School situation is that the teacher is appointed into the legal employment of the Managers and they are therefore in a position to exercise quite some influence on her security of employment and this is a matter which you must bear in mind in deciding on any course of action which involves them, because if a disagreement with them becomes a real battle then the results for you might not be very acceptable. I am not discussing the XXX that this should be so but merely stating the facts. I am anxious therefore to help you to deal with this situation as easily as possible. I think it is true as you say that some of the Managers are friends of yours, but there are at least two who are fairly hostile in their comment. What is certain is that they were entirely united about this particular situation and they stated that in this matter they were not being led by the Vicar, their Chairman, but were quite unanimous in their decision. I can assess this situation well enough from experience to feel certain that what I have just said is true and I think it is quite possible that if the battle continues they might become united in saying 'if she does not accept the Managers' decisions then she must go'.

Mr. Syer tells me that he contemplated resigning as Chairman. I have dissuaded him sine this would do your position very serious damage in the village.

I remain convinced that he is not your enemy and that he has no real animosity towards you. I have also endeavoured to convince him that you were not hostile to him personally and that all that is really happening is a failure of friendly communication between you. Indeed I have suggested to him and he has agreed to come and talk to you and see whether you and he can reach a friendlier basis of operation. I talked to him at length about the fact that a good Vicar, a good Headteacher, and a good Doctor, working in harmony, usually produced a good village. I don't know anything about your Doctor but I think the other two people in this case are really good people who are not seeing eye to eye. Mr. Syer was perturbed about the suggestion that the £20. Claim would mean fewer facilities for the children, the withdrawal of their outings etc., and if I were you I would try to avoid pursuing this line. I am perfectly sure that the other Managers would appreciate a friendly 'let's rub it out and start all over again' gesture on your part. This is what I would like to see happen in the best interests of the school.

There is one other point; you may well feel that the answer to all this is Controlled Status, Mr. Syer made the same suggestion to me on Friday morning, and it may be that some such course will be taken by the Managers at some time. It would however have no immediate effect on the financial situation, because change of status would not enable the Managers to contract out of loans already made to them and still due for repayment.

If there is any other direction in which you think I can assist please say so. I hope I have said nothing which leaves you feeling that I do not properly understand the situation, and I hope that the trouble will soon blow itself out completely.

Yours sincerely,

W. Easton

Mrs M. C. Ridout,
Whitechurch Canonicorum C. E. School,
Bridport.

P.S. I advise you strongly against taking a public line that if the school is to raise £20 the Managers can jolly well raise the rest of the money on their own.

School House
Whitechurch Canonicorum
Nr. Bridport, Dorset.

May 29th. '61.

Dear Mr. Easton,

Thank you very much indeed for your letter. I really do appreciate all you say in it, and I hope that you will forgive me if I do just add this post script to the whole affair.

I could not help feeling annoyed when I read that I was to be responsible for raising £20 a year as a sort of payment for the cessation of the dances. If I had never lifted a finger to help the Managers I could have understood this. But in all the efforts to find the yearly payments I have been the chief instigator, and born the brunt of the work. As I live on the spot it is inevitable that I am at the receiving end for sales of every kind; the children and I always prepare the room for whist drives and other events. The proceeds from the dances have never been for the school, except from the last dance held here. In Feb. we held a 'school week' – and with the help of four of the managers we raised £57, again a great deal of the work fell to me, and yet in the report of the work in the Parish magazine, Mr. Syer wrote that the events had been organised and carried out by the Managers. I couldn't care less – I don't do the work for recognition – but I quote this to show you that Mr. Syer isn't really fair to me. If he had been he would never have suppressed the letter from Canon Maples in Sept. '59 in which was stated the inadvisability of holding the dances, and also one from the Education Officer stating that the floor was in no suitable condition. These were never shown to the Managers, and I wish you could have heard him over the phone when I suggested that the Managers should be informed of both the official opinions.

I feel very strongly that if he and his wife had ever shown the slightest amount of personal friendship to me that this situation would never have arisen. When they came I had great hopes as they are of my own age, and I thought, with similar interests. They came to tea here with Mrs. Lennox and myself, and everything seemed to go very well. I certainly talked of the need for youth work in the parish – I had been taking rounders matches once a week, but I didn't feel that was enough. Since then Mrs. Lennox has said that I was too enthusiastic. That was three years ago, and since then they have ignored my existence – as far as possible. For two terms Mr. Syer didn't come into the school and after that it was only two or three times a term. We concluded that schools weren't in his line, and time and again we gave him the benefit of the doubt over his paltry excuses. I wanted to say to him, 'Look here if you don't want to come in and take the Scripture that's alright by us – only we'd just like to know' – but I never did say anything as he is so easily offended. After three years we know him – I can't help telling you that apart from the Sunday services they do no work in the parish at all. At first we put it down to his not very robust health, but when we know that he has plenty of energy for a pretty full social life, we can't help feeling a little sceptical. We know that he is plausible and personable and it took us a very long time to find out what he really is made of. Even now, I feel far more sorry for him than anything else, that he is a real square peg in a round hole, and that he suffers accordingly. His wife is cold and very efficient, and I have never been able to establish any sort of contact with her.

June 1st.

There was a good deal more to add to this – but there isn't any point in making things worse. Mr. Syer never came to see me, and I wasn't surprised. However, he came in to take the service (and thereby hangs another long tale which I won't bother you about) so I made the effort and asked him to talk to me in the house. I ate another large slice of 'humble pie', and the outcome was that we did in fact decide to rub things out and start again, and we shook hands with what I hope was real good faith on both sides. He warned me that I might find one or two of the Managers a little difficult, but I have told him that I would help to find the money as I have always done. If they sack me after all that I shall go through life a very embittered woman...

The picture really isn't so gloomy. One of the Managers is feeling very embarrassed I know. She has a daughter here who has just won the one scholarship awarded annually to West Bank School, Sidmouth. (I have to include this just to give myself a little moral boost.) However with a good deal of tact on my side, and a little good will on theirs I think we shall pull through. But goodness me, no wonder teachers prefer County schools...

Yours sincerely

M. C. Ridout

1955 – The School at Whitechurch – 'just 19 pupils'.
(Judith on extreme left of front row.)

1958 The School has grown!
(Two 'helpers' in the background.)

1957: Headmistress and student Daphne
who joined us for a year.

1992: Reunion of pupils attending
The Village School from 1955 – 1964

The School in 1963
32 pupils and 2 staff – ideal

February 2000: Margaret and Helen revisit
Whitchurch Canonicorum

Another Decision

Throughout the following years an uneasy truce existed between school and Church. No more dances were held and the schoolroom flourished as a school. The building itself was kept in good repair although renewal of the floor was never effected. Possibly another disruption to the school was considered to be unwise!

The amalgamation of the old Senior Schools with the Grammar Schools into an integrated Comprehensive system caused many problems in *that* situation. My personal response to the change was one of relief. I could never approve of an arbitrary selection policy related to the chronological age of a child; and in the village situation it was socially as well as educationally divisive. The tendency to categorise ability, learning and achievement according to age still pervades systems of thought relevant to Education and employment. The Open University has done a great deal to break down some of the conservative and conventional ideas entrenched in our educational system. Available education for all throughout one's life is a reality to be valued and pursued!

The school continued quietly to flourish with reciprocal visits with the two other schools in the area and to centres of interest outside the boundaries of the school and village. A. N. Whitehead's phrase 'the seamless robe of knowledge' was evident – I hope! – in all the busy activities in which we engaged.

I knew however that it was only a question of time before the school would be closed. Plans for an area school to be sited in Charmouth was under discussion. In theory the amalgamation of three village schools, each only three miles apart, seemed to make sense not only in financial terms but in the essential educational requirements to provide more teachers for an ever expanding curriculum

The area school was to be sited on the playing field adjacent to the existing school. In my opinion it was not the most suitable location. The small town was growing in popularity as a seaside resort and the school was situated on the narrow roadway which led to the beach. It was busy enough even in those days, hazardous for young children and would be further congested by the increase of school transport to and from the other two villages. Possibly the availability of land had been the deciding factor in the choice of site. Personally I thought that Wootton Fitzpaine would have been preferable. It was remote from any main road and with Church and school under the patronage of the local Squire it's likely that land would have been made available for such a project. However, such decisions were made at a level removed from that of the teachers of the schools involved.

The area school would be completed in five years time. Mrs. Lennox and I realised that we would either be employed as assistant teachers in the new school or would need to think of alternatives. As the plans for the building became available I realised that the organisation of the 150 (approx.) children would be in the traditional one year/one class format and knew that I would find it difficult to compartmentalise my work with the children into one yearly segments. Ongoing continuity was essential to maximise development in all the learning and growing skills required of young children. Changes of voice, of conduct and expectations cause a block, brief or otherwise in the learning process and I had worked with young children long enough to be convinced that the way we had worked in our own village school was preferable for all concerned.

Mrs Lennox thought the same and when the appointment for a second teacher in the Roman Catholic school in Chideock was advertised she applied. The school had a good reputation and was well supported and maintained by the Church.

There was another sad leave taking in our ranks. Auntie Mary, friend and caretaker, became ill and was to die of cancer.

Mrs. Woods, head of W. F. Village School applied for and was appointed at Headmistress of an Infants' school in

Dorchester. My own future as wage-earner as well as an educationalist had to considered. There were not many options available to a 50 year old woman. I *might* be considered for a Headship of an Infants' school or for the post as deputy head in a Junior school. (At the time of Comprehensive reorganisation many heads of the old Senior schools were re-deployed as Heads of the Junior schools so that few such posts were advertised.) However, that would necessitate a return to the one year/one class situation in one of the 'institutional' schools (the conveyor-belt system I called it!). I was also aware that I might not find it easy to work with a Headmaster who could well resent my unorthodox teaching methods − and my 'opinions' which I would find difficult to suppress!

My attention was drawn to one year courses for teachers being offered by the Schools of Education attached to the Universities. I had always read widely on my own account. Tillich, Fr. Huddlestone,, Bp. Robinson, Ernest Jones on Freud, Jung Bronowski, and potted versions of the philosophers published by Penguin were amongst those who fed into my obsessive 'need to know'. The thought of a whole year to study under guidance revived all those suppressed enthusiasms I had felt when the offer of a year at the Sorbonne had been granted.

I knew that it would not be possible and yet in fact it became a reality.

I was offered a one year's leave with salary if I should be accepted on one of the Diploma of Education courses. I applied to Bristol was interviewed and accepted. The supply teacher who lived in Bridport would take over and I would continue to have the use of the schoolhouse.

The family?

Giles ages 17 years had decided to leave school at the end of the summer term. He had joined the Merchant Navy with Elder Dempster in Liverpool.

Judith was in the care of two sisters in Charmouth, one of whom had worked with handicapped adults. She would return at weekends with me at the schoolhouse. It worked well and the Misses Theobold were great allies.

Helen was accepted as a weekly boarder at La Retraite School in Burnham-on-Sea near Bristol. She too would return with me to Whitechurch at weekends.

I lived in an old van on a farm in Failand on the outskirts of Bristol and returned home with Helen and Judith at weekends. I was caught twice for speeding but was given kindly treatment by the police!

It was a wonderful year which opened doors in my understanding of all I had read and experienced. There was a great team of tutors with the leadership of one Hannah Berry. I was especially interested in the work of Hirst and Peters et. al. in the area of philosophical thought and enquiry into the principles, policies and practice in Education.

There was no formal examination but assessment was based on the twelve assignments of work completed through the year – in my opinion a more valuable method of assessment for the student than the one-off examination format.

Changes involve the need to make further decisions and towards the end of that memorable year in Bristol I began to consider the options available to me for the last ten years of my work as a teacher. Continuation in the village school was not an option. Numbers were dwindling as rumours of closure began to circulate and parents began to send their children to the new area school. I would be deployed elsewhere.

I decided that the Headship of an Infants' school was not for me and, as already stated, I would not be suitable to work with children in a formal situation.

I had no subject based University degree and so was not eligible to apply for specialist work in Secondary Education. I would have been considered for remedial work with the 'slow learners' but I was not really interested and not temperamentally suited for such work. We had to have a house and I had no resources to negotiate for a mortgage. I began to consider residential work in the private sector of our educational system.

Would the Dip. Ed. qualify me to teach in one of the Training Colleges – (now University Colleges). I conferred with the tutor in charge of the philosophy course and he immediately reassured me that with my experience and the Dip. Ed. I would be most suitable; and I knew myself that to work with students hoping to become teachers is what I would choose to do given the opportunity.

I filled in application forms to Caerleon and to Kirkby Fields in Liverpool. I was called for an interview in the Liverpool College and after two very thorough interviews by the Principle and the Governors I was appointed as lecturer with a special responsibility for the 'new' course in philosophy of Education and for a course of introducing literature in Junior schools. I felt enthusiastic and competent to undertake both.

To live and work in such a situation would provide such opportunities for discussions on ideas and theories with colleagues as well as with the students I would hope to guide and to share my enthusiasms.

The campus itself met with my approval! The large area adjacent to the Leeds/Liverpool canal provided space for the ten 'blocks' of wooden constructions left over from a temporary Malaysian College erected during the war. There was a central administration block with a tower from which was a grandstand view of the racecourse at Aintree! The 'blocks' were separated by stretches of well designed gardens with pathways where I could imagine how pleasant it would be to stroll on summer evenings. The 'blocks' themselves were flexible and functional. Some were fitted out as study/bedrooms, others as lecture rooms of varying dimensions. I would have the luxury of a study where I could house my books and a larger space for tutorials and seminars.

In my opinion such low cost buildings with interior walls which could so easily be demolished or re-positioned to suit the changing needs of the community were preferable and more 'cost-effective' than the rigid and pretentious structures built to impose rather than to meet the needs of those who would work there.

I made the decision to move from the picturesque village in west Dorset to the somewhat squalid area of Kirkby on the edge of Liverpool without hesitation and without a doubt that it was the right move for the family as well as for my career. I was given a rent free 2-bedroom flat in one of the residential 'blocks'. Judith would go to a day centre just down the road from the College and Helen would attend the local C of E

Primary school. Giles was following a navigation course in Aigburth. We would all be together, practical problems were solved and with one last regretful wave to the village school and to a good friend who had come to help me pack, we set off for the next stage in our busy lives.

Part 2

February 2000

Whitechurch
Canonicorum re-visited
National School 1840

It was 45 years since I had first sat in my old Austin 7 and viewed the stone and flint building where I was to spend the next ten years teaching the local children and living with my family.

I looked at the words engraved on the block of concrete set into the south facing wall; they were a solid reminder of the purpose for which the school had been built. There was a more elegant sign carved into a suitable segment of wood positioned above the original engraving simply stating:

Village Hall 1971

I sat comfortably in the car of a friend who also was interested to see how that village had changed over the years. The boundary wall separating the school playground from the road had been demolished to make for easier car parking access and the building now stood starkly adjacent to the narrow roadway. The long Church-like window had been replaced by standard double-glazed units and the two lobbies, one at each end, had been incorporated into the main building. I walked across the car park to where the schoolhouse garden used to be but it had been erased and reduced to a patch of grass on which were a couple of children's swings. From there I could see that the old bell steeple on the end wall of the school had been retained. The School house, set along the north side of the main building looked dreary and in poor repair. It was empty, awaiting the occupancy of a caretaker. Through the window I could see that the door which used to lead from the kitchen into the schoolroom had been blocked off and I thought how inconvenient it would be for a caretaker to exit on dark winter nights for the purpose of locking up the hall. The rooms were very small and I wondered how as a family we had all fitted in!

By comparison the interior of the hall itself looked very presentable and well cared for with a splendid stage set into the space between the one-time lobbies on the south side. Our old upright piano had been replaced by a Bechstein grand and covered with a colourful drape. The north wall had been re-lined eliminating any trace of the so-convenient door connecting house to schoolroom. A ceiling of tiles covered the old rafters and suspended globes of electrical lighting ensured that there would be good light on even the darkest of winter days. The whole place had been wired and a succession of radiators had replaced the old tortoise stoves.

A new floor throughout looked sound and durable. I wondered if the worm-eaten joists also had been replaced. A block of toilets had been built on to the east end wall with access from the interior of the hall. The old urinal with the earth closet at one end had been demolished. I muttered a hope to my friend that the moderately sized septic tank sunk in the field below the school all those years ago was able to cope with the excess usage incurred by such events as the public dances for which the hall was now used. After a discreet enquiry I was told that there was no mains drainage through the village and that there was a restriction on further building. I had seen many new houses and a sizeable holiday complex on the site which once had been a farm and thought that such restriction had been somewhat delayed!

Our old workroom leading off from the north wall was now a very well equipped kitchen so that Harvest suppers must surely be far superior to the old cold meats, spuds, salads and cider feasts of past years.

In one corner of the hall there was evidence of a small playgroup. A few children's drawings were attached to a wall but there was no evidence of equipment; maybe it was all tidily stacked away! It was obvious that the hall is well used; tables and chairs were stacked in what used to be the lobby where the juniors once hung coats and hoops. I glimpsed other equipment such as bowls and a mat; all adult entertainment was well provided for and no doubt the transformation of Schoolroom into Village Hall is appreciated by most. The old Reading Room which might have been extended and renewed to provide for similar functions has disappeared.

And the children? I understand that there are approximately 16 children aged 5-11 years from the village and the surrounding area who would have started their formal education in the village school are now transported daily to a grand new school in Charmouth. The original area school which was being proposed while I was still in Whitechurch was to be sited on the playing field behind the school in Lower Sea Lane. We toured around and found only a housing estate in evidence. No doubt the money from the sale of the land had helped to finance the attractive new building at the end of the 'lane' near to the sea. It's a delightful site but I wondered about traffic problems generated by school transport and the volume of holiday traffic now that Charmouth has become a popular holiday resort.

As for the children? I ascertained that there are at present 172 pupils and 7 staff; not a bad ratio with 1 teacher to approximately 25 children. The 'conveyor belt' system is in operation with the children grouped by age into 6 classes with one of the teachers being responsible for children with 'special needs'. It's the usual pattern.

I am left with an impression of splendid buildings which have little to do with the actual needs of young children leaving home to be organised, disciplined and initiated into a formal system of 'education'. It is a further example of a system of learning being imposed from without when all serious and informed educationalists know that learning and love of learning is powered and motivated through a child's curiosity, experience and gradual understanding of this 'seamless robe of knowledge' which is his/her heritage.

I return and remain more than ever convinced that small local schools can provide better conditions for the gradual and ongoing learning experiences than is possible in the massed centralised schools where children are grouped by age into one-yearly classes with a succession of teachers.

Schumacher's dictum that 'small is beautiful' in terms of grouping human beings for purposeful activities has always made sense to me. Research based upon studies in business and industry has conclusively stated that people working in small groups are more motivated to achieve and to flourish than those of similar abilities and background do in large institutions. This applies even more significantly to the schools in which young children spend most of their waking hours.

Small locality schools, separate from the community yet integrated through local support, mutual interests and shared amenities can ease the transition from home to school for young children and the moral imperative implicit in the daily conduct of the school as a community within the large community lessens the possibility of conflicting values and standards between home and school.

It is interesting to note that in the large Secondary schools where there are problems of behaviour and absenteeism and where individual children are 'statemented' that extra tuitional help is provided so that 'difficult' pupils work in small groups with an adult; and that even a one-to-one provision is made for certain of these 'statemented' pupils. I understand that in such situations the problems tend to diminish.

If the ratio of pupils to adults was significantly reduced overall from an early age in any school might not some of the problems which erupt in later years be reduced?

My own initial reaction 'just 19 children' with whom I would work over a period of 5-6 years made more sense to me than working with one age group of 25-30 children (if I was lucky!) for just one of those fluid and formative years.

There are problems as the previous account of my own experience exemplifies. There are ongoing problems related to an ever-expanding curriculum, to the imposed straight-jackets of 'standards' and inspections, to the whole system of a careers' structure, to the education of the teachers and to the appointments system for teachers in such schools. There are problems related to the functions of school Managers, of Advisors and Inspectors... Problems are seldom resolved but get people talking and thinking, an ongoing process hopefully leading to understanding and co-operation. In the large institutionalised schools where such discussion is limited or formalized, problems tend to grow rather than to diminish and a situation of stasis arises in which there is no movement towards solutions becomes evident.

I end with my repeated conviction that small local schools can provide the stable and supportive situation for young children in which they can grow and thrive. The rest will follow...

In 1992 a reunion of all pupils who had shared with me – and my family – those ten years of working together in the village school was held, not in the School which is now the Village Hall, but in the warm atmosphere of the Five Bells, the village pub. It was sad that there were a few gaps, Ethel Lennox, Auntie Mary and Mrs Rendell amongst them.

I was very moved when a stalwart man of middle years gave me a great hug and said, 'You are a part of me.' I could only reply that he was a part of me also.

It's always such a great joy to hear from them even though there's sadness also to hear of those who have died.

I took a tape recorder and persuaded my 'pupils' to record their names, their and any memories they might have of their time in the Village School. I have that tape and it cheers me up greatly in my declining years!

I enclose part of a letter from Sally... which records memories of her time as a pupil in the village school. She was the eldest of five girls and as she writes, she was not an easy child but she was very intelligent and a joy to teach. The whole family emigrated to Australia and I have been loosely in touch with the parents ever since. Sally has spent her life working with the Aboriginies – and for them – and is held in great esteem.

...re your last letter gave me an added impetus to write. I feel very fortunate to have had these formative years at Whitchurch School and to have been taught by you. I remember so clearly your energy and enthusiasm and also your encouragement and belief in my abilities which cannot have been easy as I know that I was a difficult child. More and more as I get older I appreciate having received the individual attention that a small school permits and also the local cultural

content within which it took place. I'm referring to the celebrations of old English customs and festivities such as the May Day celebrations; going to the top of the St Candida tower on Ascension Day and looking across the vale; learning to ring hand bells; being introduced to Thomas Hardy who remains a lifelong love. The increasing uniformity of Weston culture really depresses me and I imagine that with the closure of the school these customs are no longer celebrated. I also appreciated the way that you gave us an awareness of the larger events happening outside the little world of the village. I have so many memories of these years – hearing about your time as a bargee and being shown the painted jugs; Folk dancing; nature walks in the fields behind the school; playing the role of a sheaf of wheat in a Hiawatha play (on the shores of); the nativity plays (including the one that I attended at Judith's school; the heated debate that used to rage in the playground about the relative merits of Ferguson and Fordson tractors (how could we have felt so passionately about it!) also pincushions and needle books which we made and which my mum still treasures; your disappointment in my lack of staying power when I decided I didn't want to finish some knitted item that I was making; those awful school lunches (I've got an aversion to Irish stew and cake and custard...!)

I was very interested to hear that you are in the process of writing about the village school in a time of change as it would help me to locate my experiences in the larger context.

As I think Mum has probably told you, I have been working as an anthropologist with Aboriginal organizations in the Northern Territory – firstly based in Darwin and more recently in Alice Springs – for the last five years. Much of the work has been to do with Aboriginal people's relationship to land (which as I'm sure you are aware is very different from European concepts of land 'ownership') which I've found very interesting. Two years ago a landmark decision was reached in the High Court that Australia was not in fact 'terra nullies' (ie:- empty) when Captain Cook arrived and that a form of nature title had existed which in some cases has not been extinguished. This had enormous implications for all Australians and has led to the enactment of nature title legislation. Next year I am going to be

148

in charge of nature title claims – of co ordinating them – for the Ngaanyatiarra Council, the Aboriginal organization I work for which is based in Alice Springs but...

Validity of letter from Sally may be checked by reference to her direct at:

22 Catherine Street
Subiaco
W. Australia. 6008
0061 8851 22069

or her parents at: Joyce & Chris Hodson

16 Orient Street
Freemantle
W. Austrailia 1662
0061 9755 3078

These are the true rewards for any Teacher who has been privileged to be so closely involved with the Education in its fullest sense, of children of all ages.

Reflections

The schoolroom was my sanctuary. I spent many long hours after the children were in bed and my husband was watching the TV in the known familiarity of my workplace. There was always plenty to be done in organising work and equipment but there was always time for reading and for reflecting not only about our work but about issues based upon articles I had read and upon some of the more interesting TV programmes. At one time I was concerned about the problems in my own 'religious' beliefs and of the prescribed teaching of 'Religious Education' on the curriculum. I was very grateful to Bishop John Robinson for his book 'Honest to God' and became very involved with the ensuing debate.

Many concerns about parental choice, comprehensive Secondary education, the status and training of teachers, the introduction of Middle schools and the viability and value of small village schools were in the headlines. I made my own contributions to the ongoing debates by writing letters and articles, some of which I have retained and consider to be relevant to the central theme of my book which is that small local schools are of more benefit to all concerned than the institutionalised urban schools where children are massed in large groups according to chronological age.

I also include a study, observed and written in 1968 when I was teaching in a Liverpool College, of two children on their first day at school, one in a nearby town school and the other from diaries I had kept in the village school. The study highlights – in a generalised way I admit – the long term effects that those first days and years can have upon the children in their motivation and their enjoyment of learning.

Further Reflections on The Interview

From my point of view:

The interview was conducted largely on personal factors with too little regard for professional requirements; balance kept by presence of the Education Officer.

Although the Managers had little knowledge of the professional requirements more general questions could have been asked in order to get the candidate talking about her work as a teacher.

Questions such as:

What reading scheme do you use? (It does not matter if they have never hear of Schonell or SRA etc. reading schemes come and go!)

Should children recite multiplication tables?

What do you think about football for the boys and needlework for the girls?

Do you think good handwriting is important?

(these days) Would you use a computer – calculators – a tape recorder – a TV in your school?

How can parents help?

A list of similar questions related to the specific requirements of the post to be filled could be prepared before hand so that the interview would be conducted on a much less ad hoc basis. *Inspectors and Advisors* could be asked for help and guidance in the preparation of such questions if necessary.

Managers can co-opt other professional specialists for the interview. I was very reassured to see Mr Easton although I knew that he had asked to be present, had not been invited. I also knew that he had interviewed other applicants previously in his concern for the future of village schools. Such a procedure, at the time, was unusual but I'm sure that it is to be recommended.

The absolutism of an appointment

The decision to appoint me as the Headteacher was not unanimous; inevitably there would be opposition to proposed changes, not only changes to the actual building and its usage in the community, but changes to old established routines and methods of teaching/learning.

(No reading round the class? No daily recitation of tables? Paint as well as crayons? No gold stars? Visits to Museums, to other schools etc.? Talking and movement of pupils – no rules of 'silence' or formalities of 'hands up' or 'hands on heads' etc.)

A trial period of a year would have reassured those antagonistic to my appointment and would have encouraged more positive attitudes to the changes. 'We can always get rid of her at the end of the year' would have restored their sense of authority and control over 'their' school.

It would also have ensure that the changes I had in mind were not too radical or implemented too swiftly without due regard to the effects such changes would have upon Managers and Parents. *Their* children, *their* grandchildren as well as *my* school!

From their point of view:

I was too competent and confident in my own area of expertise so that the only way in which the managers felt competent to assess my suitability was on my personal circumstance. They would have resented my obvious reluctance to discuss my personal situation, especially as it was so contrary to their conservative expectations of the teacher and her background. An ailing husband they could have accepted without too much difficulty but Judith, mentally handicapped, would limit the attention, time and energy required to teach the other children., I knew that Mr Easton also had his doubts and, had there been other suitable applicants, I would not have been successful; but in 1955 advertisements to fill the teaching posts in village schools were endlessly repeated in the Educational

Journals and it was only in the 60s that the policy to close small schools was so widely implemented.

The confidence in myself to cope with a family as well as the school obviously convinced the Managers – albeit with reservations – that it was possible.

I was positive and enthusiastic about being in charge of the village school; my qualifications were more acceptable than those of other applicant's and I was supported by the Education Officer. Support for the appointment from another source of expertise would have been more convincing for all concerned.

The Vicar and the two elderly ladies (well educated themselves in the Independent System) had been the most articulated and perceptive in their comments during the interview and afterwards. The farmer's wife, used to WI and parish meetings had also been practical and common sensical in her questions and in voicing her doubts about my ability to cope with a family as well as the school. The Captain 'bumbled'; the farmer and the builder were solidly in opposition to my appointment. I was the 'bossy' woman who would be difficult to manipulate. Feminism was not yet overtly recognised although, in such villages, the dominant mother figure was always a threat to the men who resented such dominance even though they depended upon it: a self perpetuating pattern which caused many problems for the young married couples as well as for myself. The opposition of the men was further entrenched by their own feeling (not explicitly acknowledged) of inadequacy at the meeting. (A gut feeling needs to be expressed in language if it is to influence the decisions of others.)

Managers themselves need to be carefully selected if they are to be responsible for the appointments of teachers in their schools. Who does the selecting?

Is the jury system of 'twelve good men and true' relevant or in accordance with the ongoing functions of School Managers.?

Should the Managers incorporate at least one member from the professional body of Educators?

Has the almost casual system of appointments by such Managers changed during the past forty years? ('I voted for her because she reminded me of my old nannie' still rankles! A friend told me that she had gained a casting vote from a grocer because she had the same surname as himself!)

The whole question of Primary School Teachers being recognised as a professional body arises from the fact that it is not a self-regulating, self-governing group of employees such as Doctors and Lawyers. Appointments made and disciplinary action taken are by administrators (who have not necessarily been teachers) and by lay-people not necessarily knowledgeable about the professional requirements or the personal /psychological attributes of their teachers. Teachers of young children are especially important in their influence, training and education of pupils during their most formative years. Appointments of such teachers require a greater degree of understanding and expertise by the Managers than is commonly found in the traditional 'jury' system.

The extension of a two years' period of training for a primary school teacher to three years and, eventually, to the introduction of the B.Ed. four years degree course, has been an effort to improve the status of such teachers in a contemporary society in which degree courses in the Universities and Colleges have become more widely available for able students. Or has it? All services in our society not directly related to the narrow concept of profit-and-loss accountancy inevitably depend upon a political scale of priorities for their funding; and therefore, such funding fluctuates and is unpredictable except in short term bouts of generosity or withdrawal. 'We pay for what we value – or we value what we pay for' seems to apply either way to the lack of provision in the State Education system and to the pay of the teachers. Comparisons with schools in the independent fee-paying schools should not, through prejudice, be ignored. By contrast such schools are maintained by a self-perpetuating system of those who value, in varying ways and degrees, the benefits of a 'good' education. The appointments – and dismissals! – of teachers are taken very seriously and are conducted with due regard to the central role that teachers are expected to fulfil in the Education of succeeding generations of children. The Managers – or Governors – of such schools, often parents, themselves tend to be professional and/or well-informed persons, more able to make rational judgements about prospective applicants than – for instance – the Managers of a

154

village school whose judgements and opinions are influenced and conditioned by another self-perpetuating system which is funded only indirectly through taxation and only casually enhanced by fund-raising efforts – usually initiated by the teachers for immediate and specific needs.

To be assessed and judged by one's peers when applying for a teaching post in the state system is a privilege seldom accorded to most of its teachers in the primary schools. Parents as Managers is desirable in theory but so much depends upon the parents themselves; upon their own experience and understanding of the qualities and abilities required for a particular appointment. The jury principle of 'twelve good men and true' does not apply. A rule of thumb based on common sense may be suitable to pass a once-and-for-all verdict of guilty or innocent but the same principle on which to base the decision to appoint 'x' or 'y' in an ongoing teaching situation leaves much to be desired.

R.E. – A Church School Community

Religious Education was of dominant importance in a school historically founded for the education of poor boys in the parish in order to provide clerks and scholars able to participate in the litanies of the Church. The historical importance of educating children (girls slowly accepted as pupils, chiefly through the Sunday Schools movement – they were more useful as domestic servants if they could read and compute!) in the religious mores and practices of which ever denominational church had founded the school became traditionally accepted even in the more 'liberated' county schools.

Whitechurch was a Voluntarily Aided Church School, affiliated by deed and practice to the Church of St. Candida. (C of E) and, as such, the Managers preserved their right to appoint the teachers who must be communicant members of the Church; for example, they must attend Church services and regularly participate in the Communion Service.

This was no problem for me as I had been reared under the shadow of the Abbey Church in Sherborne. None more devout than I during all my growing years and, although doubts and judgements directed at the institution of the Church had surfaced in my mind during more recent years, I was still convinced that a religious framework for the development of moral awareness and spiritual sensitivity was essential for us all in this tricky business of living our lives.

Each day started with the obligatory Morning Assembly followed by the Scripture lesson based upon a syllabus issued to every Church school in the Diocese of Salisbury. It provided comprehensive guidelines for Bible study, for instruction in Prayer Book services and Church history and an annual inspection by a member of the clergy would ensure that I was doing my 'religious' duty.

Parables, the Miracles, the journeys of Paul, Moses and Noah (of the Old Testament) et.al. had become over-familiar to the older children through the previous years and my own references to Biblical wisdom were always interpreted in a wider context than that of historical and parochial events.

Father Borelli and his work with the urchins of Naples, Dr Albert Schweitzer and Lambarene, Father Damien and the lepers, Mother Teresa (and the other Teresas, of Avila and Lisieux) were among my patron saints at the time (religious inspiration as evidenced in their lives gave meaning to the more abstract study of Biblical truisms) and we supported them with zeal, with prayer and with donations. Lent was a good time for encouraging self-denial in order to give pocket money for worthy causes! We read, recorded, illustrated acts of courage and fortitude in our own time. Gladys Aylward had led a large group of orphans form a missionary school in China to safety across mountainous and uncharted territory during the Communist purge of religious institutions. She was a working-class girl who had been 'called', 'inspired', to work in China as a missionary and had overcome prejudices of the 'Church' against her background and lack of formal education to achieve her mission. Was she deluded as Joan of Arc may have been? I did not think so at the time and all my later doubts seem irrelevant when related to the lives and actions of those 'inspired by God' who, in turn, inspire us lesser mortals to 'go and do like wise'.

Larger events beyond the confines of the village community – the assassination of President Kennedy, a royal wedding – were included in our thoughts and prayers during those morning assemblies. The overlap of history, geography and other related subject areas led us in many directions but always (I hope) with reference to our central core of religious belief and practice.

The association of great paintings, sculpture, architecture, poetry, music with religious inspiration did not come within the pages of the official R.I. syllabus but could hardly be ignored. Our continuing, if often erratic, progress of discovery into the inherited wealth of our culture enriched the narrow concept of R.I. as defined in the syllabus. I belonged to a music club from which I brought a monthly LP record at a discount price and which was played on my daughter's record player while we ate our dinners. 'Nymphs and Shepherds', tuneful arias from the operas, the Gelineaux psalms sung by the monks of Downside Abbey (and which we aspired to emulate!) and excerpts from the great orchestral works helped to deflect attention from the less savoury of our school meals.

With an increased understanding of the inter-relatedness of knowledge I placed emphasis on Religious Education rather than on Instruction which reduced the syllabus – in my eyes! – to a programme of lists to be memorised and of stories and anecdotes isolated in an historical past. R.E. is so much more than teaching the bare bones of such a syllabus just as Education is so much more than teaching the bare bones of the 3 R's. The skeletal frameworks need flesh and the spirit of imaginative and informed understanding to give them life and a meaningful relevance to this 'tricky business of living'.

The assemblies were not always so serious and earnest. We sang hymns with great verve and enjoyment. I remember that the Crimond version of the 23rd psalm (the Lord's my shepherd) – with descant! – was a favourite. The chants of the Gelineaux psalms were tuneful and repetitive with refrains in which we were able to participate. The psalms are poetry and insist on being read aloud – more grist to my articulation mill.

As a Church school we were also aligned to events in the calendar of religious occasions; Christmas, Epiphany, Ash Wednesday (and pancakes on Shrove Tuesday!), Good Friday, Easter, Whitsun (and a week's holiday at the loveliest time of the year!), Harvest and then Christmas again. The nativity play – with variations and additions! – was an annual event enjoyed by parents and friends. A stage was made from flat-topped desks grouped together and covered by my old bedroom carpet, cheerfully dragged into the schoolroom by the stalwarts. On Ascension Day we all trouped to the Church. Volunteer mothers looked after the younger children while the Vicar and I shepherded the others up the narrow winding stair to the roof of the tower where we sang hallelujah hymns and looked for landmarks in the village spread below us. The parapet was too low for my ease of mind and I was always thankful when a shower sent us scurrying back to rejoin equally apprehensive mothers! The Church was a friendly and familiar building in the early years of my appointment as the village schoolteacher and we used it as central to our local studies and as the pivot round which revolved many of our activities. We decorated the niches and ledges with the abundance of spring flowers which grew in that sheltered corner of Dorset. At Harvest time it was traditional for the children to decorate the east transept with their offerings of fruits and vegetables. There were weddings and christenings and funerals, bell-ringing occasions and Sunday-school activities so that there was continual interchange of visits between Church and school and with teacher and Vicar united in their common concern for the Education (in its widest sense) of the children. Sadly, this was to change when the Vicar retired through ill-health.

Meanwhile, the good Canon came into school every Friday morning to take, or to join in, the assembly and to give instruction to the older children (8-11 years) while I busied myself with the younger ones at the further end of the schoolroom. He was always interested in the individual children and their work, gave me support and encouragement (even when he disagreed with some of my more 'liberal' ideas!) and we were always glad to see him.

With some trepidation I undertook my commitment to 'take' the Church choir. To 'take' meant that my role was that of intermediary between the Vicar, the organist and the choir. The organist was a competent and unassuming lady who understood the idiosyncrasies of individual choir members and of the organ alike. All were well versed in the traditional rendering of familiar hymns, psalms and responses and all I did was to arrange the venue for the practices (when the weather was cold we often met in the schoolroom warmed by the two large tortoise stoves. Auntie Mary was also a member of the choir and ensured that we met in comfort!) and to act as arbiter when there was controversy over the choice of chant or hymn tune. I also enjoyed singing in the choir and to do so, my own children Giles and Judith, sat with me in the back row of the choir stalls – one of the first of many departures from the accepted practices in school and Church into which I was often provoked by my (then) unique personal situation. Members of the Church community were very tolerant and accepted Judith's occasional escape from the choir stalls to join some friendly face she had seen in the congregation —usually during the sermon!

During my first two years school and Church trundled along easily together. The Diocesan syllabus was adhered to – with additives – and we were well prepared for the annual Scripture Inspection Day when one of the Church dignitaries came to interrogate the pupils on the content of the syllabus and to assess the teacher's moral and religious influence on the children.

The dignitary assigned to our village school was a retired clergyman of indeterminate age and with an indeterminate interpretation of his role as an inspector. He stayed for the whole day, arriving promptly at 9 am in a hired car which I was informed would call for him precisely at 4 pm.

It was hard going! He had no set programme and said that I should occupy the younger children while he tested the older ones on their biblical knowledge. As the morning wore on, surreptitiously I digressed from the religious theme to give extra individual reading tuition while I engaged the rest with drawing and other 'quiet' activities. I lowered my voice to an approximation of the serious religious tone which I noted was in vogue at the other end of the classroom.

At 10.30 am on cue, Auntie Mary came to the rescue with coffee and our Inspector seemed quite content to relax. A conducted tour around the garden with a discreet indication of the boy's urinal lengthened the break to half an hour while Auntie Mary stayed on duty to prevent any infringements of such unaccustomed freedom.

During the lunch break – school dinners which we ate with the children – I put on a couple of records on my daughter's gramophone; Bach and Handel I believe! The afternoon session was relieved by much hymn singing and by a further lengthy break for tea and biscuits.

After that first experience of a 'Day with the RE Inspector' I prepared the day's programme in advance with as much variety of occupation for the pupils that I could devise. When a second teacher was appointed to the school we referred to the event as

'Entertaining the Inspector' and our efforts were well rewarded by reports couched in superlatives! We all enjoyed the day, reading, reciting, illustration (our own illuminated ms.!) enacting prepared Biblical scenes, singing, dancing even (round a golden calf realistically drawn, painted and mounted on an easel!) with the younger children joining in whenever possible. Our Reverend visitor was an appreciative audience to all our efforts made on his behalf to ease his role as Inspector and, if at first, I had bristled at the whole idea of such an inspection and then resented the 'performance' which I felt impelled to devise, I soon began to feel sympathy for his Reverence at being appointed to such a sinecure for which he had little aptitude. After all, what did it matter? Any break in the daily routine of work was welcome and any visitor from a different environment helped to create an effective diversion from our own inward concentrations.

A Church School

Doubts are integral to any belief especially when that belief is put under pressure.

I had accepted the allegiance of School to Church almost without question. Historically the School had been founded by the established Church of England. The Church had been a centre of pilgrimage since the Middle Ages and the Shrine, presumed to contain the bones of St Wita – or St.Candida – still is maintained. The saint was a nun who joined a group of missionaries with St Boniface in France and was martyred. The name of the Village itself is interpreted as the "Seat of the Canons." With the good Canon in charge I had no reason t doubt or question our allegiance to the Church.

With the change in the leadership of the Church the whole question of the roll of a Church School and of my responsibility for the religious education surfaced in my mind.

The moral imperative implicit in living as a community was based upon Christian principles but when there was so little support for the School from its progenitor and I personally dissociated myself from the affairs of the Church, I began to question the validity of Schools controlled under the jurisdiction of religious authority.

In the present political situation when denominational Schools still exist, for immigrants as well as for traditionalists, further discussion as to the advisability of retaining such Schools seems to be imperative.

Inevitably other questions must be asked.

In a secular School is there a missing dimension? We talk about educating the whole person and that to include the spiritual sensibility however that may be interpreted.

Is there a system of ethics unassociated with religious beliefs?

Fundamental philosophical and political questions need to be explored if there is to be any considered alternative provision of a system of education to suit the needs of all our children.

Programmes on television often provided subjects for discussion between the teachers and often between teachers and parents who shared our interests. Dr.Schweitzer was one of our 'role models' and when his work was so criticised on a popular programme I felt impelled to write on behalf of us all.

The second letter was to a Dr. Goldman and was written during the Billy Graham crusades in this country.

The letters are included to indicate a wider reference of interest and enquiry into the questions arising from the teachers' responsibility for Religious Education in a Church School... The content was shared by pupils as well as the teachers and letter writing was an important item in our curriculum.

Letters

In defence of Dr. Schweitzer

Whitechurch Canonicorum
Nr. Bridport, Dorset.
April 21st 1964

Dear Mr. Michelmore

No doubt I should address my remarks to a certain Mr.
McKnight – but I write to you as it was in the 'Tonight'
programme that the adverse criticism of Dr. Schweitzer and his
methods were projected. There will be many to write in the
doctors defence I am sure; but what disturbed me was that there
may be many thousands who by this presentation will
misunderstand Dr. Schweitzer's motives.

I have no doubt at all that Mr. McKnight was justified in his
criticism of the lack of sanitation and modern equipment at
Lambarene. Other men have visited the hospital in the same
spirit of sceptical criticism, but they have returned with a real
understanding of the work being done, and not with the
superficial criticism based on western standards of modern
hygiene. I suggest in this respect that Mr. Mc... studies the
methods of sewage disposal and the water supplies in some of
England's rural areas, and he'll not find such very wide gaps
between them and Lambarene.

To come to the point... The whole crux of Dr. Schweitzer's
belief 'reverence for life' cannot be illustrated as the rather
senile idiosyncrasy of an old man careful not to destroy even an
insect in a glass of water; it is the positive realisation and respect
for the natural order of all created things, and the complete
interdependency of the animal and plant word evolved by
millions of years of trial and error. This is what the Doctor in his
wisdom and humility understands so well and for which he has

far too much respect to disturb and upset. Recently we have seen all too clearly how man in his arrogance has seriously disturbed this careful balance with the irresponsible use of his poisons and experiments in a world of which he understands so little.

The second point against the Doctor was on the grounds of the poor sanitary conditions and the lack of modern equipment. No doubt to a clinically minded doctor sterilised even of human understanding, the whole place must seem to be the very antithesis of the wards of starched beds and scrubbed patients where even the homely smell of disinfectant is an irritant. Dr. Schweitzer recognises that a man's body cannot be separated from his mind and spirit in order to receive medical treatment. He did not go to Lambarene as a great white chief to impose the sterile clinical methods of western standards and habits upon his African patients. He lives amongst them as one of them, accepting their conditions of life, their families and their cooking pots, their scabby animals and friends who accompany the patient to the hospital so that he shall not feel cut off from his background, or frightened, suspicious or unhappy. I quote from his book written in 1930 – 'The indifference of the primitive man towards persons he does not know is beyond anything we can conceive.' Even our modern psychologists recommend that children in hospital should be cared for by the mother when possible.

As for the use of canoes instead of the motor boats advocated by Mr. Mc... I would suggest that the answer is the same. The natives prefer the quiet efficiency of their canoes to the noisy churning of the motor boat – and who is to say that they are not right?

The arrogance of the western world in supposing that it understands the rightful meaning of 'progress' leaves me in much doubt when I see what havoc this progress has caused in Africa. It is impossible to impose another culture upon a race of people – however supposedly inferior, or for whatever misguided good intentions – without their full co-operation. To impose different standards, habits and religions from the outside can only cause chaos, anger, misunderstanding and untold harm. Any help must, with humility, be offered through love, from the inside. The two great men of our age in Africa who live out this fundamental truth, are Dr. Schweitzer and Father Huddleston.

I hope that one day Mr. McKnight will come to understand this, and perhaps he will write another book about Lambarene...

Yours sincerely,

M.C. Ridout

Whitechurch Canonicorum
Nr. Bridport, Dorset.

Jun 19th. 1966

Dear Dr. Goldman,

I was very interested to hear you speaking on the 'Meeting point' programme this evening, especially as I had sent for inspection copies of the work cards based on the concept of life themes. To be honest I was disappointed in these; the theme programme starting with the day to day experience of the child and developed to include biblical teaching and possibly symbolic interpretation according to the understanding ability of the child, is not anything new. Many teachers have taught in this way under the old heading of 'projects' when especially related to the RI teaching. The cards certainly synthesise the themes in a practical way, but I personally think that they are too expensive and not very artistically produced. This of course is not of primary importance, but the cards have to compete with well illustrated books produced at a comparatively much less cost.

You will forgive my criticism I hope. It is so good to hear of people genuinely concerned about 'religion' in its real sense and especially those concerned with the leading and guidance of children and young people.

I so agree with you when you spoke of the need to strengthen the intellectual sinews of our thinking about religion and its implications for the individual, and I'm sure that this attitude is the one chiefly required for talking with young students and reasonably intelligent adults. But I was sorry to hear that you think Billy Graham has done much harm. He too was on 'Meeting point' and after listening to him I remain convinced that he has a very special role to play in the particular society of our age. The emotional appeal is there, but backed up by deep thought and his understanding of the people to whom he speaks. I was impressed to hear him say that man cannot come to God headfirst – not even heart-first (as he might well have said!) but with the whole of himself. He reminds me very much of the colourful glossy magazine out to sell the goods. And as this is what a large section of the population has been conditioned to respond to, perhaps this is just one way to help arrest some of the apathy and indifference. We are in such an age of transition that several layers of perception must be acceptable before we can all move towards the maturity of a truly religious community. I know too that Billy Graham teaches a very literal acceptance of the Bible and there is the eternal danger of the Law transcending the Spirit; but I see such masses of people not only without Spirit but without Law also, who are driven before any prevailing wind which blows, that I have come to think that the Law is better than nothing, and that for them who never progress beyond the literal and concrete concepts of living the scaffolding is still necessary.

That the emotional appeal can so easily deteriorate into sentimental rubbish I also agree – unfortunately we see all too much of this in the schools – I might add that such societies as the Old Sarum Fellowship have only aided and abetted this particular attitude in the 'holy joes'. But there is always the possibility that some will win through the emotional appeal to glimpse the realities. Many women become arrested at the emotional level, noticeable not only in their religion but in their treatment of children and animals generally, and in this age of scientific precision with its demands of empirical proof perhaps we have erred a little in the other direction so that all emotion is suspect. Freud was a man of extremely strong emotions – perhaps inspiration only comes through intensity born of strong emotion? That it must be then checked and put to the proof by all the intelligence available to us he proved every time. (God, give me a bigger brain?)

I was interested in the remarks of the children – am I wrong in thinking that they are from Piaget's observations in Jean-Jacques-Roseau Institute? Or possibly they were from children with some sort of religious background. They would not be typical remarks of children coming to school at five (no statistic available to day!) as we find that children of this age, even if they have heard of God, have not heard the word 'heaven', let alone that parable of the prodigal son, so that the problems of wrong concepts begin with the advent of school, and its ensuing effect. And the only hope of doing anything about it is to 'move'

167

in the Colleges of Education... a decision I also reached about 3 years ago! (I am going in October to the Bristol Institute of Education precisely with this aim in mind.)

Thank God for the 'Southwark crowd' and all others like them; thank God too for the television which gives us all the opportunity to listen and meet with like-minded people; and especially thank God for paper-backs and people who write for the common man...

No answer required. I just felt like writing as there are two women here who have been talking and thinking along much the same lines as yourself, although with many more limitations of training and ability.

Yours very sincerely,

M.C. Ridout

The 11+ entry examination
to the Grammar School

Controversy over the type of secondary education based almost entirely upon the results of standardised testes in English, Maths, and an intelligence test was growing more overt among the more liberal intellectuals concerned with state education. The word 'comprehensive' was in the air. But I was grateful for the 11+ as it represented a yardstick by which my competence was measurable by those whose judgements was limited to such factual evidence. So long as I 'got them through' whatever else I did, or did not do in the name of education was acceptable. And, in those first two years the number of pupils who 'passed' was acceptable – at least to the parents concerned.

I was not averse to such selection but only to the ensuing results. Entry to the Grammar school was prestigious for parents as well as for pupils. (Sheep and goats, I used to think; but why were sheep considered to be more prestigious than goats?) The problem centred upon the alternative provision made for those who did not pass the 11+. The old Senior schools offered only more of the subjects already taught in the Primary schools but with no incentives such as GCSEs to work for in order to influence possible employers. Many of the teachers in such schools were demoralised, second rate teachers compared with their University educated teachers in the Grammar schools, and the pupils were resentful, first for having 'failed' and then for being confronted with a further three years of dreary instruction. If only there had been comparable provision of Secondary education for those who did not go to Grammar school. The Technical Colleges provided many excellent courses in subjects such as tailoring, catering, plumbing, carpentry etc. but were available only to post-school students. The three-year hiatus in the Senior school was all too often a discouragement for most to continue any form of further education. A further check for entry to a Technical College was the lack of provision, at least in our corner of the country. The only one was in Weymouth,, 30 miles distant, and with no public transport, a student would need to be lodged with friends of family – if such existed – during the term.

Eventually the Secondary Modern Schools replaced the old Senior schools. A syllabus with a wide and varied choice of subjects to provide a more liberal secondary education with opportunities for taking O.N.D. and H.N.D. qualifications. This would complement the narrow academic curriculum in the Grammar schools. Enthusiastic and well qualified teachers were attracted to such schools which often were purpose built and with facilities and equipment provided to cover the courses on offer. But the provision of the Secondary Mods. was localised and there was only the old Senior school in Lyme Regis for our pupils.

When a comprehensive system for secondary education was introduced and the 11+ exam was abolished in many parts of Dorset as elsewhere, tensions and acrimony between families in the village, within the families and between parents and teachers diminished.

'If only you had been here last year,' I was told. 'Our Sheila would have passed.' The complement, acceptable at the time because of my own need for approval, professionally was inadmissible. It was small wonder that many teachers in small schools taught narrowly to the prescribed material gathered from tests of previous years in order to ensure the maximum number of passes. Their reputations depended on such results. Even in the town schools it was known that the 'best' teacher was given charge of the top class in the Primary school. The curriculum was restricted and tailored to equip pupils only to pass the standardised tests in the basic subjects. Such subjects as Music, Dance, Drama, Crafts and Art and most creative activities were regarded as 'frills' and irrelevant to the real aim and purpose of education in most Primary schools. A thorough grounding in language, numeracy and penmanship had its value but, in itself, was limiting, repetitive and often discouraging to the natural curiosity and creative need to experiment and experience which is so evident in the growing child. (Does there have to be an 'either/or'?)

With release from the strictures of the selection tests innovations and experiments in teaching methods and curriculum content began to flourish and I, for one, welcomed the change.

However, for those first two years I had reason to be grateful for the 11+ as the 'successes' offset suspicions about my then – unorthodox teaching methods – no rigidly timetabled lessons, subjects diffused into projects and classes dispersed into flexible groupings – and my even less conventional family background.

Comprehensive Education
and
Parental Choice

With reference to 'I know my rights' in the programme 'You and Yours' presented by Nancy Wise on Wednesday May 12th 1976.

The discussions on a comprehensive system of education for 80% of the nation's children continue on the same parallel lines of argument with no sign of a bridge to meet the requirements of either side. On the one hand we hear eminent educationalists putting forward the social/political and somewhat questionable educational rationale for the full implementation of comprehensive education and, on the other, there are the parents who are not convinced by the clichés and jargon and who remain unhappy and vociferous about the specific schools to which their children are required to attend. From their own observations they remain convinced that their children will not achieve their potential in academics, skills, social living, creative and aesthetic awareness, even in daily behavioural standards; nothing they see of the schools reassures them; not even the impressive buildings, the academic degrees of the teachers, the art displays or the long euphemistic speeches on formal occasions or the less formal reassuring banalities by teachers in the formal settings of P/T meetings.

The arguments have reached stalemate while government policy continues to implement – although rather more hesitantly of late – the comprehensive system for 80% of the nation's children. Parents might be rather more reassured if the policy referred to 100% of the nation's children.

They might also be reassured if, in fact, parental choice was a reality instead of a mythical clause in the 1944 Act which, in practice, is totally meaningless. Choice implies alternatives. While children are massed in large monolithic institutions and the zoning principle is adhered to there are no alternatives. Massing the nation's children into large imposing edifices may impress certain sections of the population, may rationalise the rewards system which is based upon morally and educationally unsound principles, may, in fact, seem to solve short term economic and social difficulties but will seldom meet the needs – educational, social, emotional, spiritual, even physical needs – of each individual child in that school. Massification implies regimentation. Educational theory which places such value upon the individual in our particular society is in direct contradiction to the practice enforced by the large school structures. Monolithic institutions cannot meet the needs of individuals unless those individuals become institutionalised. It depends on what we want for our children – Orwellian society with the 20% in control or a society of 'free' responsible, critical, thinking individuals?

Has no-one read Schumacher's 'small is beautiful' – a study of economics as if people mattered – or the mass of de-schooling literature which is becoming strangely prophetic? His thesis that people are happier, work better and demonstrate active, positive and creative attitudes in small groups and enterprises is significant for educational structures as it is for success in industry and business. If the schools remained as small units so that each individual – pupils and staff – could know and be known, so that parents and all interested parties could participate more meaningfully in the whole life of the school, the barriers of suspicion and mistrust by the parents would be channelled into constructive reciprocity of advice and information and the defensive retrenchment of teachers in the anonymity of large institutions would necessarily dissolve in the daily business of knowing and being known by all concerned with, the growing and learning of another generation.

The paradigm of the old village school embodies the true meaning of comprehensive education and in the good primary schools this structure still exists. With good teachers, more interested in the development of their pupils that in their own promotion and the reward systems, this basic principle of 'small is beautiful' might bridge the gap between a comprehensive system and parental criticism. It might mean that materially ambitious heads would go elsewhere to satisfy their needs for material gain. I wonder if any Head of a large school can justify his appointment on either educational or ethical grounds?

The old argument that young adults require a greater diversification of teachers and resources that a small school can provide is irrelevant. Most schools already make use of the public library, the theatre, swimming baths, visiting speakers and so on. It is extremely wasteful for schools to monopolise the use of large and expensive resources which would be better centralised for communal use rather than regarded as the prerogatives of a particular school. The prestige of a school has been known to be enhanced by its acquisition of a swimming pool or an athletics track... What a situation when four schools in a small town each has to raise money for its own swimming pool, none of them open at the weekends... In an age of easy transportation would it not be better to pool resources of teachers and equipment for the benefit of the whole community?

Instead of an institution to house 2000 pupils why not four schools for 500 pupils? Each school could provide the diversification, the general and the specific teaching required by young adults. The aims of a large school are so multifarious that confusion often results for staff and pupils. A clear statement of the philosophy, aims and procedures which a particular school embodies might help parents to make a 'right choice' for each child. A school would have to earn its reputation. The Head of an independent school once said to me, "If I don't make this a good school I lose my job. My school governors are as interested as I am in the well-being of the school and they ensure that I earn my pay". That a statement of policy and aims and values should be reflected in the actual practices and ethos of the school, if it is not, reputation is lowered, possibly lost until restored by more genuine and sincere staff. Four separate and individual schools are more likely to offer diversification of curriculum, character and 'specialisms' than one large and unwieldy institution can hope for. It would also make 'parental choice' a meaningful proposition.

Many independent schools are truly comprehensive, fees being the only criterion for entry. Parents who pay can choose. Problems of geographical location are overcome by a boarding component. I want my child to have a good musical education because this is her area of interest and ability. Apart from the fees I am prepared to send her to a school in Manchester where her needs will be met. Many other parents would be prepared to do the same if the general principle of parental choice could be exercised without a purely financial criterion for entry. Specialist school and general schools – we need all and every variety. Parental choice is a legal and moral right in this country and, until it is made possible, the wave of discontent will grow, and the monolithic institutions will become as irrelevant and redundant as the churches. I would not necessarily need to send my child to Manchester if the local monolith was broken down into manageable units one of which could well offer my child all the advantages of a specialist education that she now receives in Manchester. Most people would prefer *not* to pay twice over for their children's education but will continue to do so as long as the state schools fail to meet the needs and expectations of concerned parents.

The greatest mistake of the policy makers was to equate Comprehensive schools with size and to regard resources as monopolistic rather than as shared and communal. The other grave mistake is to turn good teachers into indifferent or bad administrators and to hold out the financial and prestige rewards to those most easily tempted.

I realise that this raises many far reaching and fundamental issues – related to social structure and political controversies. But the large comprehensives are not reassuring especially to the parents, the smaller ones in rural areas seem to be more successful. Smaller units each with its own clearly stated identity might be a move away from the real disaster areas for staff and pupils. The whole area of appointments by knowledgeable people, the rewards structure, the voucher system of payment for education, studies of how teachers work are only a few areas of investigation – and of course, there's always the Union...

M.C.R.

Competition

Competition and co-operation are mutually exclusive concepts.

In recent years I heard of a primary school teacher who abolished all the competitive elements of work and activities in her work with the children. She was fiercely criticised on the media and, sadly, she did not counter the accusation that she did not prepare the children for the real world where they would need to be competitive in order to survive. The same criticism was levelled at me many years previously when I did not have regular tests with lists of marks displayed for all to see, did not award gold stars etc., did not encourage competitive games. (Competitive sports have a slightly different connotation and are restricted to those with specialised interests and skills.)

Our sports day confirmed my own conviction that competition between children, even between those of roughly the same age and ability, is to be treated with caution.

Competition implies concepts of success and failure which determine developing attitudes in relationships and achievement (or lack of if). Within the 1 imitations of school experience success and failure are mostly related to academic ability and/or gamesmanship; and success or failure in either capacity has a tendency to be cumulative – 'nothing succeeds like success' or, 'I can't win so why should I try!' Either way there are built-in deterrents to the development of what grandly may be referred to as 'the fully integrated self'. Attitudes of complacency, intolerance, arrogance even may be fostered in those who are always at the top of lists or who win all the prizes whereas, attitudes of diffidence, insecurity and a sense of inferiority are speedily developed in the continual 'non-achiever', especially in the younger child. Rewards and Punishments are concepts closely allied with success and failure. Does the teacher always reward those who succeed (lists, stars, preferential treatment etc.) and punish (withdrawal of praise, verbal criticisms and abuse etc.) those who do not measure up to standardised tests and achievements? All too often in the transient transactions between 30-40 pupils and the teacher during the brief space of one year this is the case.

Encouragement for the slow learner is only possible in the one-to-one relationship and over a period of time. Most children learn in fits and starts, depending upon many factors such as interest, health, emotional stress, physiological and cognitive development.

Tests – such as are devised by those not directly involved with the teaching of young children – are educationally irrelevant to any real assessment of a child's learning progress.

We cannot escape the moral dimension of teaching despite the efforts of some who would treat it as a business concerned only with the input of information and its utilitarian function.

I could not avoid the moral implications of competition, not only on sports day, but in the day-to-day work of the school. No-one works in isolation even when closeted with a computer screen for hours at a time.

Attitudes of tolerance, concern for others (or otherwise) affect relationships at every level. The competitive aspect of behaviour is derived from the 'survival of the fittest' primitive response to a hostile environment.

In the schoolroom there needs to be a restraint upon this constant need 'to win at all costs'. Working – and living – together in project work and any combined operations requires degrees of tolerance and mutuality which modify, even exclude, the competitive drive of the individual.

To work for the common good is, of course, an ideology which cuts across the competitive cut and thrust of capitalism. You take your pick! but one hopes with some understanding of the ensuing effects on the individual as well as for the society. I came down heavily on the preference for fostering co-operative attitudes in the schoolroom. In any case, the competitive drive to succeed in most individuals is strong enough to survive the modifying influences of a philosophic teacher! It might be remembered that the 'real world' referred to by the critics of the

177

teacher who abolished competitive activities in her school is only a very small part of a whole wide world influenced and determined by ideologies other than our own.

Whitechurch Canonicorum
Nr. Bridport, Dorset.

16.5.63.

To Sir Edward Boyle,
Minister of Education

Dear Sir,

Along with thousands of other teachers I have watched your helmsmanship with a very wary eye. We have had such a succession of Ministers, none of whom seem to have been more than aloof, disinterested figureheads, that naturally we are rather sceptical of anyone who accepts the job. Perhaps I am mistaken, but it seems to me, that you are one of the few to have taken some real interest in the schools and the work that goes on in them, as well as being involved in the endless financial wrangles.

Primary schools are enjoying a slight boom – for the first time ever. At last it has been recognised that all further education depends entirely upon the basic groundwork of education in the first six most important years of a child's school life. And now there has been frantic scurrying to refurbish the face of Primary Education, smarten it up, and bring it in line with the flashy new Sec. Mods. I can't help feeling as I watch the frantic efforts to make a good show on insufficient money, that very often the real *sordid* problems of Primary Ed. are not even touched.

Being 'inside' the job, and having taught in many and various types of schools, I feel that some of the problems I have met with have been partially or completely solved in this small country school, and I felt that I could not keep quiet about what I know of Primary school education in this transition period of upheaval, unrest and discontent amongst the teachers today. I am convinced that the discontent is not only from financial causes, but from conditions in the schools themselves.

I rather suspect that in sending this paper to you I am not 'going through the right channels'. As I have no notion of what

179

these channels might be, and as far as I can judge from hearing you speak, you seem to be the one who is interested, and who has the power to get things done!

You must have dozens of reports from all your many advisors but perhaps one from a teacher who has tried the practical approach of certain theories, may be of some small help. I send it only with this in mind.

Primary Schools

'To think that I used to love teaching.' These are tragic words from a still young teacher who is trying against almost impossible odds, to retain her interest and enthusiasm in what should, and could, be the most absorbing, varying and interesting work – that of training and guiding the coming generations of children. For personal reasons she moved from teaching 16 children in a small country school to take a class in one of the town's 'child factories'. The attitudes of other teachers on the staff can be summed up in their own remarks:

'The moment that we've paid up the mortgage on the house and car, I'm getting out.'

I'm only teaching to help put the boys through University.'

'Only two more years, thank goodness.'

'I'd give anything to change my job, but I've no qualifications and it's too late now.'

And so on; typical remarks, not only from this school, but from thousands of others up and down the country. What effect can this attitude have upon the children, being taught day after day by resentful, tired, frustrated, mentally and spiritually withered teachers? The answer is too frightening to be considered too deeply; and yet this must be done, or we are a lost race of people.

For the past eight years I have worked in a country school as a conscious experiment to try and solve some of the problems which confront people who take up teaching. Some are physical, and a good many are spiritual.

Physical problems

There is one that we all know and recognise – the impossible numbers of children in the classes. It is quite impossible for an adult to know and teach more than 20 children at a time. It is impossible to teach any child until a sympathetic link has been created between that child and the teacher. This usually is established in the first week or so of the school year – but not always. There are the few with whom it takes much longer, requiring more thought and patience from the teacher. In classes of 30-40, the links between the teacher and these 'difficult' (only difficult because of conflicting personalities) are never formed. There isn't time; there isn't the nervous or emotional energy to spare for them. And so for a year at least, these children are not 'taught' – in the real sense of the word. 'Streaming' will not help; even if there are 36 'A' children in a class, the link between the teacher and each child still must be formed before any real progress in the child's development can be made. This is essential, especially in the Infant and Primary stages of a child's school life. Children cannot be massed together, as in adult classes, to be 'instructed'. Initiation and development through all the complicated processes of acquiring knowledge is highly personal for a young child, and this of course is only one aspect of education. Each child progresses at an individual rate in each subject. How can one adult hope to give individual help to 30-40 children in the 8-10 subjects taught in the Primary School? Here begins the sense of frustration; the work towers like an unscaleable mountain. The teacher, always in its shadow, can only hope to clamber up the first foothills. As energy and hope diminish the teacher sinks back into the shadows of apathy, and often bitterness.

In this small country school there are 30-36 children aged from 5-11 years of all ranges of ability, and two teachers who have the same ideas about educating the young. During the six years that the children are here, we feel that we really 'know' each child, its special difficulties, the home background (this is especially important) and what each child is potentially able to do. I have never had a child here with whom I have not been able to establish a sympathetic contact, although in four cases it took well over a year to do so. (Three of these were children who came here from other schools at later ages.) Work in Maths is almost entirely at individual speeds. Teaching in English is entirely fluid, groups of children forming and re-forming according to the grammatical needs or the varying interests in Literature and drama. Each child knows that I know what he or she is trying to do all the time; this helps their confidence in breaking new ground, and it also 'stretches' him to full capacity. To discover the potential in each young child, to draw it out, make the child aware of it, to fire an enthusiasm in his ability to

182

discover and create, are the great opportunities of a teacher in a primary school. However, if the material is presented in such overwhelming quantity the teacher can only treat it as a shapeless mass, recognising only the awkward corners and the one or two hopeful leaders.

The 'One class – One year' method

3rd Sept. Miss…, 36 seven year olds from the infants. They are yours until July 31st with the exception of the two holiday periods. After that you can push the whole lot up to Mr…, and after he has 'handled' them, they pass in to the next class, and finally into the class of doom to be regimented on the great sorting parade ground of the 11+ in charge of the fiercest, grimmest looking teacher of them all. His reputation hangs on the number he 'gets through' each year. No corporate effort this; for some strange reason Mr… always takes the 11+ year, and for an equally illogical reason he is held responsible for the 'results'. Four years in the Junior school, four teachers, each grimly closeted with his class for a year, in a light airy room if he's lucky, with 40 children in a 16ft x 16ft opening on to an noisy road and with one half of the room in Stygian gloom, if he's unlucky. Perhaps there's an extra teacher to take the 'backward' children, damned and stigmatised from the start – but he's only too glad to sort out some of the 'weeds' to make his own burden a little more bearable. There's a Head somewhere around, who prances through a morning assembly, and then is seen no more, except perhaps to demand why the whistle is two minutes late after morning break, or what is Miss – doing outside her classroom during lesson time. (No-one is allowed an irregular bladder!)

This is the beginning of the 'factory school', teachers and children being pushed into their allotted grooves, the human irregularities forced into the concrete pattern of progression. Teachers become hysterical, they have breakdowns, they are constantly red-eyed and heavy-headed from incessant colds. They are always escaping through illness or through marriage, or, if they're lucky, through a Headship and finally if exceptionally lucky, through retirement. The war of course provided a wonderful 'escape route'. As for the children – well we know too much these days of social problems.

Why this rigidity?

The five teachers at such a school were the clever children of their grammar schools, taking advanced academic courses in one or two subjects at least in their subsequent college training. Why isn't this extra knowledge fully exploited? The only subject which has to some degree always been treated as a specialist subject in the primary schools is physical education. I know that in some primary schools, and certainly in almost all the newer schools teachers do specialise in their own subjects; but there are still hundreds of schools where it isn't even attempted. A teacher who has no musical sense at all prefers to use the BBC lessons (and very good they are) rather than make the necessary adjustments for 'her' class to be taken by another teacher. Sometimes of course, the physical limitations of the building are to blame – but more of that later.

It seems to me that in a subject such as Maths, it is absolutely essential that it should be taught throughout the whole school by one teacher only. We all know how greatly the methods and language vary from person to person and from school to school. As far as possible a Head will try to standardise the methods used in a particular school, but there are plenty of individualists who will always think that their ways are right, and who will not conform. And what about the children? One teacher talks about the difference between numbers, another about 'taking away' and another about 'subtraction', three terms for one process. One teacher 'adds a ten to both lines', another 'borrows a ten', and another talks mathematically in the new Cuisenaire style. Only the 'brighter' children will be able to follow some sort of rational progress through all the complexities of language and method used by teachers from varying backgrounds. It would seem to be obvious that one teacher for Maths throughout the school would solve many problems. And of course, so with the other subjects. We all teach better the subjects in which we are really interested.

Another important asset to this specialisation is that the

185

teacher now has four years of 'knowing' the children, and of retaining daily contact with them. Continuous, harmonious contacts with the children spaced out over four years are of greater and more lasting value to teacher and children, rather than the isolated concentrated one yearly period when the children must suffer inevitably from the daily undiluted diet of one personality, and the teacher forces herself to endure the same four walls endeavouring to cope in all the subjects set on her timetable with the 40 energetic youngsters whose only common link is the fact that they were all born within the same twelve months.

'Streaming' in the bigger schools

This is suppose to help the teacher in schools where there are hundreds of children who are all sorted and graded into A's, B's and C's. Some teachers are supposed to enjoy teaching the C groups. I never did understand how and why teachers were selected for the A groups, but in some mysterious way they were always regarded (certainly by themselves) as superior to their fellow teachers. I taught French in one such school – with the A stream of course – and was therefore, in my own silly estimation, a head and shoulders above the others – and I believe this to be a fairly common attitude. As for the children – it's obvious isn't it?

'I'm a 'C' child – I can't do anything – I don't care – I won't do anything – Right, I'll make a bloody nuisance of myself,' etc. etc. Can you blame him? Who wants to be a 'C', or even a 'B'? And even if the children are so graded, in each grouped class there are still 30-40 different individuals all needing individual attention. The usual question asked of a teacher in a country school is, 'However do you manage with the enormous age range?' The answer is simple – the right number of children. All effective teaching is based on individual help and tuition, projected into small groups when advisable. It doesn't matter if the age range is from 5-11 years and if the abilities range through A-C; there are no such divisions in the small school, and no comparisons. Each child exists in its own right, and can develop whatever gifts he may possess to their full

186

limits – because the teacher has the necessary time for his particular needs. Children here do not grow up feeling inferior – we do not have 'problem' children. (At the moment we are 'carrying' an ESN child. He takes his place – is excellent at 'sewing' as he calls his craftwork – and he is not a social misfit.) From such a school there are far less likely to be social misfits and delinquents as there must be inevitably from the 'C' streams of the larger units.

This leads to physical disability number 4 – these enormous units of 200-1000 children, maybe more – but the thought is paralysing. More and more 'factory schools' are being built – accommodation for 'n' number of children. Frightening and bewildering the first term or two must be to any 5 year old, used to a family unit of 4-6 persons. Next term's intake will be 45 – this in a local town; and only one teacher to cope with nose blowings, lavatory visits, dinners, milks, lunches, shoelaces, homesickness, fear and bewilderment. In the small units most 5 year olds are well acquainted with the teachers and the school. They can visit on the odd afternoons to meet brothers and sisters, or children of the neighbours. The transition from home to school is achieved without any sense of suddenly being cut off and lost in a sea of unfamiliar faces. The building is smaller, he or she knows his way around, and throughout his primary school life he is very much an important individual contributing to all the school's activities. If he must join a larger unit later on he is more able to 'take it' – in the early years he has built up a confidence in himself and an attitude to work which will take him anywhere.

Why do new schools have to be built in such dimensions? Surely it would cost very little more to build 4-5 units instead of the one great factory?

In this rural area there are many two-teacher school, and a few one-teacher schools. On the one-teacher schools there is little comment – it depends so enormously on the one person concerned. Personally I ran this as a one-teacher school for 18 months, and was very happy; and until there were more than 20 children I felt well able to cope. But it depends so entirely upon the temperament and character of the individual concerned that such a person needs to think very carefully indeed before attempting such a job.

We work now, very well indeed, as a two-teacher unit with 30-36 children between us. The one snag is, that being so similar in our opinions and interests, we do not complement each other in the subjects taught. We do not find this a very great disadvantage as there are so many excellent aids available these days to help the teacher in her less able subjects. For instance, I find the TV programmes on Science and Geography invaluable; and to break any monotony of my presentations we use BBC programmes when and how they fit into any particular scheme or project.

But, the two-teacher school does not seem to be altogether satisfactory. So often there is the odd child working through alone because there is no other of similar age and interests in the school at the same time. For instance, at the present we have a school of 24 boys and 10 girls, and one girl in the top group has worked right up through the junior school with three boys who obviously tend to group together. There is no other girl anywhere near her age with whom to talk and play – and this seems to be the great disadvantage in too small a unit. From the teaching point of view the primary (5-11 years) school seems to fall into three main groups, and with only two teachers the 'middle' group often seems to get a bit 'left'. In a school of 60 children and three teachers, we feel that a better job could be done. Any unit of 60-100 children with 3-5 teachers would be the ideal unit from every point of view.

Buildings

Maybe the 'factory' can afford to provide the gymnasium, the assembly hall, the stage, the swimming pool and the playing fields. It also seems to afford an incredible number of unnecessary luxuries, which I secretly think are rather for the benefit of impressing important visitors than for providing aesthetic backgrounds for the children. All that children really need – is space – plenty of it inside and outside; and teachers would like the necessary equipment. What's the use of mosaic floors, murals, statues, splendid gym apparatus, mirrors and even furnishings, when the children constantly have to be reminded to 'take care'? Primary school children are energetic, noisy and rumbustuous. The first time that I saw this school, it looked like an old barn, 90ft long and 30ft wide, no paint and no decorations – but the one requirement – space. Now of course we have paint, bookshelves, a slide and such equipment as the miserable capitation allowance permits. Children can move freely from work bench to reading corner and work groups without knocking elbows and causing minor commotions. It would be better still if there was easy access to the outside, but this is not such an essential. We have no fine gymnasium, but sufficient (almost) equipment for all of them to mobilise and strengthen all and every muscle. We have a spare room used for school meals, which can be cleared quickly and used in bad weather. We have no assembly hall or stage, but the room itself is soon transformed into concert hall, and the grouped desks covered with a large carpet make a surprisingly stable stage.

Playgrounds seem to consist of large areas of bare asphalt, scrupulously litter free and unimaginative. Compare these with the grounds of prep schools. We do not ask for acres of lawns and streams and playing fields, but surely there could be some compromise. Grass, trees, walls, hedges, corners for children to hide in – indestructible boxes and planks for building. Grass needs cutting we are told – we have plenty of boys well able – and willing – to push a lawn mower. There's a 15-20 minute break morning and afternoon and usually ¾ hour for most of them at midday. What are 36 energetic, enquiring youngsters supposed to do in a garnished, walled-in square of asphalt? And also, there are summer days, when one of the joys of living in the country is to be able to work outside. But there's no shade, and a row of desks on hard, sun-reflecting asphalt is no pleasant change from a cool, airy classroom. I cannot think that an imaginative scheme for playground planning would involve much cost.

Headteachers

Everyone knows that any unit in any sphere depends upon the leader; and nowhere is this more obvious than in the schools, where children walk in orderly rows and where the teachers look as if they have forgotten to laugh or even smile, is a sorry reflection upon the Head. But this is not extreme picture – very many primary schools emanate this atmosphere. What is the Head's part in this? An absolutely major one.

How is the Head teacher appointed? He or she has worked through a requisite number of years in not too many, and not too few, schools, and finally works in post labelled 'special responsibility' before being considered a 'suitable candidate'. He must look fairly presentable, be able to express a few ideas on religion, text books and staff management, and he must appear confident. A year's teaching abroad and extra school work such as leading expeditions in the holidays, will help.

Why does a person want to become a Head? In some few cases it is for the real reason that he feels that he can make a good job of it. But so often it is for far less worthy reasons. Many men are driven to apply for financial reasons – the demands of a growing family cannot be ignored. A Headship also means that he has a study to himself – and in a larger unit, he can escape from the burden of classroom teaching. He can now usefully employ himself on timetables, form-filling, seeing workmen, welfare officers, school meals' officials, medical and dental officials, officials from the 'office', and occasionally the awkward parent. He can organise jumble sales, fetes, parent-teacher meetings, open days, country dancing rallies, music festivals, sports' days, demonstrations, educational courses, educational visits, concerts, holiday camps, evening classes, etc. etc. – all of course to be undertaken by his already much overstrained staff. And his staff get through the days waiting for the holidays, waiting for their chance to 'escape'.

But none of this seems to me to be the essential work of a Head teacher. In the smaller units, he is still in charge of a class, so that most of the suggestions for out-of-school activities go into the waste paper basket.

A woman applies for a Headship usually because she is

ambitious, sometimes for the extra money and the prestige, and sometimes because she has ideas about schools and education which she would like to put into practice.

There may be other less conscious motives for prompting a person to apply for a Headship – these are not for me to speculate upon. She usually follows the same pattern as her male counterpart, except that she insists upon 'discipline' as much from the staff as from the children, that she is usually 'pernickety' about all the details of the whistle-blowing, correct posture, orderly walking, noise in corridors, knocking on doors, and the strict conservation of stock behind locked doors. She is usually very touchy about any infringement upon her authority and position. So, immediately there are two camps on the staff – the head v. the staff, or the head and deputy v. the rest. Superficially there are staff meetings to discuss curriculums, difficulties and events. More often the staff is presented with a programme of events which they will be expected to carry out. Real teaching problems are shelved or glossed over, and the year's work is often left to the individual teacher to prepare with little or no reference to the work of past or ensuing years. If the head does give out the schemes of work, they are often ones that can be bought from certain sources, or they are old, over-worked schemes which bear no relation to the present needs and variations. Here I must stress that there are the exceptions – the good heads who do a really conscientious job, saving and helping their staff, and despite great difficulties, welding the school into a happy united consciousness of character and work.

But too often there seems to be too little time or interest on the part of the heads to prepare the real work of the school. It is too much left to the individual teachers who may or may not bother about working to any consecutive plan. As long as the results are acceptable – that's all that matters, What are these 'results'? Very often purely superficial ones. The 11+ results are of course, all-important. In a 'poor' year the staff is rallied and scolded and goaded to make more efforts. The human material involved seems only to be thought of in terms of statistics. Other 'results' often demanded are to be seen in the good impression created by decorating the classroom – plenty of pictures, practical arithmetical apparatus, a nature table, preferably with an aquarium, a selection of pictures and friezes executed by the children. Perhaps even a model; a selection of 'tidy' books to be used for showing people, a few original poems and one or two exhibition essays. Now all teachers know that these things in themselves, and truly participated in by the whole class, are admirable. It is in fact what can be done with 20 children, but which is almost inevitably 'cooked up' by the teacher for effect when he has 40 children who must all be taught the basic necessities for further learning. We all know that teachers choose, put up the pictures, supply a good deal of the material for essays – almost write the wretched little poems themselves, and almost hold the children's hands to produce the necessary works of art. We all know that junior children make bookshelves dreadfully untidy and that apparatus is soon disarranged if really used by children. Junior children cross out, write hurriedly, turn up the edges of books, break off pencils, use incredible combinations in their experiments with colour, and generally 'make a fair mess of things' in their enthusiasm to get with something in the exuberance of production. A 'tidy' room with 40 tidy desks, and its immaculate shop window display can soon be effected as we all know, by the teacher staying after school to do it. The results of primary school work do not seem to me to be quite so cut and dried – and I think that they are best seen in the child's attitude to work during the first year at his next school, be it a grammar, comprehensive or modern school. All children at the primary stage should have learnt to enjoy school, should have had a good introduction to all subjects in as wide a range as the staff is able to provide, should have learnt to follow a line of interest on his own without any direct supervision or pressure from the teacher, should be able to work whether or not the teacher is watching, and should have a sense of responsibility and a critical appraisal towards his own achievements. This may sound a little pretentious, but in a school where the children are working individually or in small groups, this attitude to work is really necessary, and to greater or lesser extent the children here do work in this way.

The adjectives which come to mind when applied to a primary school Headteacher, are scarcely flattering. At best they seem to be benevolent despots, with idiosyncrasies of speech and mannerisms stamped firmly into them, making them ready targets for caricature, ridicule or even venom. The heads of other types of schools don't share the same fate to quite the same degree. Why should this be? These people started off at 20-22 years with as much enthusiasms, energy and interest as any other intelligent starting out on a career. What goes so sadly wrong in the work which needs all of these qualities, and more, all of the time? So much hangs upon the Headteacher. There is so much he or she can do to help the 'lesser brethren', to help out with the actual teaching, to see where some free time is badly needed for heavy marking or work on a special product, and to step into the gap, to know the children, and where possible the parents also; to co-ordinate the abilities of the staff; above all to keep the staff as happy as possible, and not to expect of them more than she is prepared to do herself; to make constant adjustments to timetables and programmes; never to be rigid and over-fussy about relatively unimportant details. "Whoever of you shall be the chief, shall be the servant of all." Always to remember that the teachers are adults, responsible for their own work, yet with their own human problems and shortcomings.

An enormous job, an enormous responsibility – yet there is *no training* for a Headteacher. He goes straight from the narrow confines of the classroom to take on a job demanding powers of organisation, understanding and ability to meet, direct and talk with all types of people, strength enough to make decisions and to stand by them, clear and unprejudiced judgement. I am absolutely certain that all embryo Heads need at least a year's training for the job. This surely could be done either at the Training Colleges, the Universities or even centrally.

Further courses in adult psychology, with special references to teaching are very necessary. From dealing all day, for years, with children, and with few contacts with adults outside his own immediate circle, he is suddenly pitchforked into dealing the adults for most of the day. Parents especially need a great deal of understanding and help; there is the domestic staff, officials and work people, and most important of all the teachers themselves who need the help and leadership of a wise Head.

He needs time – away from his job, to decided just what his Headship is about, what it involves, and what shape his day to

194

day work will take and what sort of school he wants it to be. He needs time to think, discuss, read and observe all aspects of this tricky business of education. He needs opportunities for meeting others in different spheres of education, to see it as a whole nation-wide (preferably world-wide!) process, and his own primary school in relation to the bigger vision. He can't do this, bogged down in his own little world, surrounded by hundreds of little jobs, many of them irrelevant to teaching. He can't get outside it.

Most teachers have little or no training in office routine. A Headteacher taking over a school has to find out by trial and many errors what all the various forms are about. There is no-one to initiate him into the mysteries of filing and recording, into the procedures for medical and dental cards, and so on, except his own common sense, unless the school is large enough to carry a secretary. The local offices must know how many Heads are unreliable about returning certain forms on certain dates, about omitting the reference numbers on letters, etc., etc. There is a whole office procedure attached to every school, and even a very short course in clerical work required by the local Education Authority would be very useful.

He needs practice in public speaking. Too many Headteachers feel inadequate to address meetings, even to members of their own profession. This is not because he has nothing to say, but that he is nervous of hearing his own voice in a hall with adults for an audience. This may seem strange when a teacher is speaking for most of the day, but it quite true that most teachers cannot seem to talk, express opinions or discuss logically and clearly in public; and this is usually from lack of training and exercise in the art. We have seen evidence of this, all too sadly, on recent TV interviews. All teachers, whether Heads or not, should have more training in public speaking. In villages and towns they are usually expected to address WI meetings, lead discussion groups, and make the necessary speeches at various functions. But there aren't so many to whom this comes at all easily.

There should be opportunities to meet and talk with the county's various organisers, to catch up with the new ideas, find out what equipment is available, and to know a little more about the administrative side of the Education Authority. It could be an opportunity for knowing one or two of the Ministry's inspectors (it wouldn't be such a bad idea to be able to meet the Minister himself during this wonderful interim year!). I feel that the value of this year could be enormous – far more important even than the present third year in training.

The spiritual background of a school obviously is far more difficult to define in a series of cut and dried points; but it is the most important factor contributing to the genuine education of the child. This doesn't have to be based on any narrow religiosity attitude, neither is it to be coerced from a formal daily observance of payers and hymn singing in the morning assembly and half-hour Scripture lesson. It depends – unfortunately – entirely upon the teachers and even more directly upon the Headteacher. The spiritual development of a child is as important as its physical and mental growth – I would say more important, as it is through the spirit of the person that his whole life is shaped.

This spiritual guiding can only be given through instruction if that instruction is fully understood and applied by the teachers themselves. It is to be seen as an all pervading spirit of love and understanding between teacher and teacher, between teacher and children, and between the children themselves. It is to be seen in the toleration of other's differences, in the attitude of the stronger to the weaker, in the recognition of the good in everyone, in the loyalty to the community widening as the child grows in understanding. It is to be seen in an attitude to work, not based on competition, but on self improvement; an attitude to work based on enjoyment of work; and a real desire to know about things; an attitude to work based on co-operation between pupil and teacher, not on the master-slave relationship.

There is no better foundation for spiritual growth than the teaching of Jesus Christ, as long as it is consciously thought about and applied to the whole business of living. There is plenty to think and talk about in these days of relentless questions and probes, and the primary school is the obvious seed-bed for the seeds of questioning, thinking and self-knowledge in which to germinate. Ethics used to be taught as a recognised subject and remnants of the subject are retained in certain schools, recognisable in the accepted codes of behaviour, the offender penalised by ostracism and physical punishment. What do we have in the primary schools? Are we 'cut off and bleeding at the roots?' or can we give the children some reason for learning, and show them how to use their abilities with some wisdom?

But the teachers need to have discovered all this for themselves before they can help in this spiritual growth in the schoolchildren. If they themselves have attended spiritually starved schools, what hope is there? I can only suggest that the answer might lie in the Training Colleges.

There is a great deal of talk and planning these days, in architecture, about bringing the outside indoors, and I feel that the same principle could be applied to our schools with much profit to the whole community. So often the primary school exists in strict segregation from the rest of the town or village, with the exception of concerts and open days when visitors are formally invited. It cannot be open house all of the time, but surely it would be better for all if there was a little more coming and going between the outside and the inside of the school. It seems that we could with great advantage use the abilities in the community more than we do. There is always the erstwhile cricketer, only two anxious to pass on a few tips to the young enthusiasts, the amateur painter who will come in for a demonstration or two, or someone who has been to Russia for a holiday and has brought back photographs and is longing for an audience – and so on. Naturally the head will have to exercise a little diplomatic discrimination, but education is so wide and varied that teachers need every aid that is available.

It seems therefore that the major problems are the size of classes, the size of the units, and the quality of the Headteachers.

I'm sure that a 'Dr. Beeching' will have to be done in Education before any real improvement will be seen in the teachers and their work, enough to induce others to come and fill the ranks. Perhaps it will be necessary to exclude children from school until the age of 7 years, and that the 5-7 year olds temporarily could be in charge of 'unqualified' – people for teaching, but well able to cope with all the physical training in social habits which are so often lacking in the 5 year olds who have not been to Nursery school.

As for the Headteachers, it seems to me that the whole framework hangs upon them, and there seem to be so few who really have any deep understanding of the job, that here lies the greatest problem. 'A tyrant breeds a tyrant', is a well know saying among teachers about their Heads. I would also suggest that rigidity breeds rigidity, and as the generations succeeds generation in the same traditions, what hope is there unless some real effective break is created, and some very new beginnings attempted.

The following letter is included to indicate how difficult it was – and still is in many situations – to bend the rules, to make an exception. I had written a lengthy report to recommend Fiona's transfer to the Comprehensive Secondary School a year early and had accompanied it with samples of her work. When my request was refused I felt impelled to make a further effort on her behalf.

The result was that I was asked to make arrangements for the county's Educational Psychologist to interview Fiona and to administer tests in a strictly private situation. I put the small workroom at his disposal and hung 'Not to be disturbed' on the two doors. Those were the days when batteries of evaluative and diagnostic tests became available to the specialist psychologists in the universities. They were mostly of American origin having been used during the war to select officer 'material' and to select men for specific work and activities.

The young man arrived, insisted that I would in no way be involved and retreated with Fiona and his tests. I was not in the least concerned. I knew that Fiona would take him and the tests well in her stride. He endorsed my recommendation without hesitation and Fiona was transferred at the age of 10 years. I missed her; she had been a joy to teach through her early years of 'schooling'.

I remember being resentful that my judgement had not been accepted although the responsibility for teaching these children had been mine for the past ten years! The validation did little to appease my indignation!

DORSET EDUCATION COMMITTEE

Whitechurch Canonicorum School,
Nr. Bridport, Dorset.

November 24th 1965

Re. Fiona Maribel Turner. D.O.B. 17.3.56

Dear Sir,

The longer I think about the decision that this child should not be considered for early entry to the secondary school, the more impossible I find it to accept.

I enclose the two intelligence papers which she completed with ease seven minutes inside the scheduled time. In a larger centre no doubt she would not be outstanding, but here she is head and shoulders, both physically and mentally, above any of her peers. She has progressed steadily at a constant and good rate all through the school, and to hold her back here for a further year can only have a discouraging and demoralising effect. It will mean a year of mental and social isolation as the only two children of her actual age group are 1-2 years her inferior in every way. She is in no way temperamental; on the contrary she is equable and well balanced.

This is the only child during the ten years I have taught here who in any respect has been a suitable candidate for such consideration, and I would not persist if I did not think her case to be exceptional.

If there are certain regulations, surely there must always be exceptions and precedents which need to be judged upon their own individual merits, especially where children are concerned.

Yours truly,

M C Ridout

Whitechurch Canonicorum
Nr. Bridport, Dorset.

28.6.63

Dear Mr Easton,

One always thinks of many more points which could have been raised at a meeting, and so I'm adding a written contribution of one or two things which might be worth mentioning. It was interesting to note that no-one raised the question as to whether or not the two-teacher school is an economical unit. It only goes to show that we aren't so mercenary-minded as some people might think.

Yours sincerely,

M C Ridout

Further points arising from the discussion on small primary schools.

***

Another point which I believe was not raised, is the fact that in a small unit of less than 100 pupils, *the Headteacher must still teach*. I consider it to be an absolute necessity that all Headteachers should be in a classroom for some good part of every day. They do not then become impersonal dictator-organisers, expecting more from individual members of their staff than they are capable of giving. A head must be *of* the community, and not *above* it, to ensure that he keeps to the front of his mind the day to day difficulties and stresses of teaching children.

The enormous rewards of the teacher in a small school

These are the rewards which the head and teachers of the 'factory' unit can never hope to experience. Rewards in teaching are not tangible products – in fact I'm sure that teachers often become cynical and bitter because there are no rewards. But in the small school there is always the reward of seeing each child develop and 'open out' in all their various ways. There is more satisfaction in knowing that one has been able to teach *every* child, and not just the top layer. There is always the joy (can be time-encroaching) of the continuous links with the child as it grows up – the personal interest in the child always remains in greater or lesser degrees to an extent never experienced by teachers in a large school. These rewards are very necessary to teachers. After all the 'out-giving', like the rest of our race, we need to the thanks of those who have tried to help to provide fresh impetus and strength for the 'feeding' of the coming generations.

DORSET COUNTY COUNCIL
COUNTY HALL, DORCHESTER, DORSET

EDUCATION DEPARTMENT

J.R. BRADSHAW, M.A., COUNTY EDUCATION OFFICER

Telephone: Dorchester 1000

YOUR REF:
MY REF: JRB/DB/315

7th August 1964

Dear Mrs Ridout,

I received your letter dated 9th July with its thoughts on the Headteachers' Conference in West Dorset and I am sorry not to have had time to reply to it earlier.

I am all in favour of giving the audience as much opportunity as possible to take part in discussion rather than simply being talked at. This was my main reason for substituting for the rather worn our 'brains trust' a session in which Heads could comment upon, criticise or even oppose points which I make in my progress report. The extent to which they take advantage of this varies surprisingly from one Conference to another, and I agree with you that at Beaminster this year people were far too preoccupied with some of the least exciting problems of selection. This was not so at other Conferences this year or last, when discussion tended to range widely and interestingly over many topics.

I do not agree with you that to split the Heads into groups, each with a spokesman to report the findings of the group publicly, would be a suitable arrangement for our Heads' Conferences. I have often taken part myself in this sort of discussion and it is always time consuming and often superficial. Moreover it requires skill and practice on the part of the reporters to be concise and fair to all points of view.

Many of the topics you suggest would be entirely suitable

for a professional gathering of teachers under the auspices of their association but I shall bear them in mind when it comes to constructing the programme for next year's Conference.

I do not want you to think that I am not grateful for the suggestions in your letter, and I should not like you to think that the pattern of the Conferences is fixed in perpetuity, but they are not convened without a great deal of careful thought here. Perhaps I might add that I cannot recall a Conference attended by the Headmistress of Whitechurch Canonicorum at which she has not spoken her opinions: the more Heads who follow her example at these Conferences the better.

Yours sincerely

First Days at School

September 1996

Two children aged 5 years begin their formal education.

Gary is of the youngest in a class of 30 new entrants. His birthday is July 30th. The school is a 10 minute walk away from the estate where he lives.

Tony is almost one year older than Gary; his birthday is October 3rd. He joins other new entrants to the village school which is just down the road from number 6 in the row of eight council houses where he lives.

Sandra Jones, Gary's mother, lives on a housing estate on the outskirts of the city. As an estate it's not so bad, far better than the high-rise flats built after the war to house people from the condemned back-to-backs in the city centre. Her gran hadn't wanted to move out. She didn't like the lift, even when it worked; she was on the 5th floor. She died of hypothermia when an air-lock cut off the central heating to her flat in a cold spell. Sandra's father was away working in Newcastle at the time. He returned for the funeral, met up with some friends for an evening in The Eagle and was persuaded to apply for work as a plumber on the new industrial estate. He met and married Sharon, a machinist, and all went well for a couple of years. With both working it was easy to get a 95% mortgage on one of the new semi's. They borrowed more money to cover the cost of furnishing and equipping their home – so many glossy adverts for 'easy' payments.

Then Sharon became pregnant and had to give up work. It was a struggle on one income but they managed. There was a second child, Sandra's brother (now in Australia).

The factory which manufactured washing machines where their father worked closed down.

'Get on your bike and look for work,' urged the Government. Their father had done just that and they had not seen him since.

Luckily(!), both children were at school and Sharon returned to her work as a machinist – lucky to get taken on, due to her past experience. Always the threat of redundancy hung over them. The house had been repossessed and most of the contents sold to cover debts. They were able to rent a flat in the Tower block where their Gran had died.

On leaving school Sandra's brother joined the Merchant Navy and emigrated to Australia.

Sandra got a job in Woolworths – the most she could hope for. She loved dancing and was successful in being chosen as one of the local team of Formation Dancing. Her mother made the costumes and they both enjoyed her success.

She married Gordon, her dancing partner who was a car mechanic by day. They lived in two storage rooms above the garage where Gordon worked – 'on condition there are no children' had stipulated the owner. Sandra and Gordon agreed; family planning was an accepted way of life in these enlightened times.

Sharon, Sandra's mother, died from cancer three years later and they able to rent her flat. 'Just for the time being,' they had said. The flat was damp and badly maintained, graffiti was everywhere and thieving a way of life for the growing numbers of the unemployed. Gordon's dad was in Walton goal for a series of burglaries. He had been employed as night watchman at a large Comprehensive School, had been 'retired' at the age of 50 – with no pension. He knew how to enter the school and there was a ready market for TV's and the increasing supply of new equipment to the school.

So Sandra and Gordon were careful. They would continue to pay rent rather than fall into the negative equity tap. Six years later they were still there. They had just the one child, Gary, all they could afford in these uncertain times.

The garage owner had diabetes and intended to retire when

his son came out of the army to take over. Gordon had never got on with the son and the uncertainty of future employment made them play safe. If Gordon was unemployed there would be help with the rent and other social benefits. BUT FOR HOW LONG?

So, on September 9th, 1996, Sandra and their son Gary joined other Mums clutching the hands of their 5 year olds on their way to the purpose-built school two blocks away where Sandra herself had been a pupil.

'I hated it,' she told Gordon when she returned from the Parents' Evening. Perhaps it would be better for Gary. The young teacher was about her own age and seemed lively and energetic. She had come back early from a work-participation holiday in Wales in order to meet the parents of her class of 30 new pupils.

There was hardly room to move and little opportunity for any talk with the teacher. Sandra did not stay.

Little had changed since 1972 when her own Mum had brought her. There had been almost 40 youngsters then in that same classroom; all glass one side where she sat —too hot in summer and freezing in winter. For weeks she had been terrified to move from the security of her seat. Some of the boys looked rough and troublesome although they were her own age and she had often seen them joining in the gangs who played on the derelict patch of wasteland near the flats. She was always so glad to see her Mum who met her from school during that first year. Playtimes and dinner times when she had to leave the safety of the classroom had been a continuing nightmare until she joined a group of other scared infants who stayed well within reach of the teacher on duty.

How did she ever learn to Read, Write and Compute? Many didn't of course.

When she had transferred at the age of 11 years to the nearby comprehensive, the fears from those early years re-surfaced. She was often 'not well' and was absent for long periods. Her Mum had not insisted – was even pleased to have Sandra at home to do some cooking while she was at work.

She clutches Gary's hand even more firmly as memories of her own past fears are revived. Not so bad for him, she hopes, he's a boy.

'You alright?' she asks.

Gary looks up uncertainly.

'Tony?' Tony is his friend. He's two months younger than Gary and has to wait for a further year before he can be admitted to the school although he can read some of the Dinosaur books already. His Mum had written to ask if he could start school with his friend Gary but the reply stated that, due to numbers, there was no vacancy. As if one would have made the difference – but the Headteacher had been adamant. There were 30 new entrants already and only one teacher to cope with all the problems of 5 year olds, starting school. She might get a helper if she was lucky.

'Got Jimmy? Sandra asks. Jimmy is his favourite dinosaur model.

'Where's Tony?' Gary repeats.

'See Tony at teatime,' she says brightly.

Teatime is a long way off for a 5 year old shut into a strange room with 30 other youngsters and with only a strange woman instead of his Mum to ask for help.

'Want to wee,' he says.

They are joined by other Mums – even a Dad or two – all trailing one or two youngsters. There are prams, groups of the older pupils chasing, scuffing, and shouting. It's a long walk for a 5 year old and Gary starts to drag.

'Want to wee,' he repeats.

Sandra envies the Mums who drive their kids to school. Gordon needs their car for work.

'Have a choc,' she says to distract him.

They arrive and are directed by a big girl to join the other new entrants in the hall. Sandra wants to take Gary to the toilets but he has wet himself already. Luckily she has brought extra pants – on the advice of the teacher on Parents' Evening.

The children are told to sit on mats and Sandra must leave with the other Mums (and Dads!). She looks back at Gary; it's such a wrench for both of them. And she's not reassured when a small girl starts to scream and another rushes to follow her mother. The mother turns back.

'Better to go,' says the teacher. 'She'll be alright.'

As she leaves, Sandra peers into the classroom where Gary

207

will spend his first year; where she herself had spent that first fearful year – so long ago. She's thankful that Gary can read a bit and count up to 20. Her Mum had been too tired to give her much help. But she had liked to read much later on – she still liked to read but it was mostly magazines, not books. And, of course there's the telly. Gary always enjoyed the puppets on Play School.

She indulges in further reminiscences as she returns to the flat, trying not to think of Gary scared and uncertain with all those other youngsters.

She remembers Julie who couldn't talk properly; who made sshushing sounds and cried when the teacher told her to be quiet. There was John who wandered about – wouldn't sit in his chair. Jean who was always wetting her knickers... and... Well, they had all survived one way or another. The teacher spoke in a funny voice and used to call her stupid when she didn't understand what was said. She had learned to recite a b c but it seemed to have nothing to do with 'reading'. She had been a slow starter; didn't get the hang of reading until she was 8 years old, in Mrs Andrew's class and there had been a student who had helped her a lot.

That was when her young brother had started school and her Mum had gone back to work. She had a key to the flat on a tape round her neck so that she and Keith could get indoors. Better than having to play outside until their Mum got home.

At the corner she turns to take a last look at the school – all glass and concrete. Not bad for the area. Only 6 classrooms leading off from the hall and only about 200 children. Some primary schools had twice as many with a 2-form entry.

Gary would be alright and the comprehensive had a good reputation for GCSE's. It was the best they could hope for.

***

At the same time in a village to the west of the county, Tony and his mother, Marion Barnes, start on the short walk to the school in the centre of the village. There is no footpath on the road and Marion holds Tony's hand. There are more cars now with the growing number of residents in the neighbourhood and Tony likes to run on ahead, not aware of possible danger.

A car does pass them; it's the wife of a prosperous builder who lives a couple of miles away. There are three other youngsters as well as her own in the car and Marion knows that parents who live at a distance from the school have grouped together to provide the daily transport of their children. She resents the changes the newcomers have made in the village and yet knows that it is mostly due to their influence that the village school has not been closed. Country cottages had been bought up, renovated and modernised to accommodate those who preferred to live in the country rather than in the towns where they worked. Her own grandfather's cottage with a couple of acres is now owned by a solicitor and his family. The extension to the cottage is twice as large as the original building and there is a pony in the paddock. The newcomers still do not mix easily with the local families. Marion knows them by sight and they wave as they pass in their cars. They meet briefly at meetings, at school and Church functions but the social round does not include her or the other village families. The Church has been repaired and refurbished at their expense and the old choir has been disbanded in favour of recorded music under the direction of a 'trained' musician. The Vicar, once an RAF pilot identifies with those who support the Church with their cheque books.

Marion lives in one of the six council houses in the village, built in the 1930s to house local workmen and their families. Marion's husband is an insurance agent and they are buying their house from the council. She and her husband had both attended the Grammar school, still surviving despite all the efforts to introduce the comprehensive system. She left at the age of 16 years with minimal qualifications. She knows that she only passed the 11+ due to the good start she had at the school where Tony will now attend. She had taken a course in dressmaking and had always made a reasonable living. It was a useful skill which she could continue to pursue at home even when she was pregnant. She regrets that there will be no more children; a bad miscarriage when Tony was 2 years old necessitated a hysterectomy. She too had been an only child; her father, a seaman, had left them when she was 5 years old. Her mother was a nurse and they had lived with her parents in the cottage which was now owned by the solicitor. Marion's gran had been evacuated from the city during the last war, had met and married her granddad who had been a farm worker. Both dead now and her mum had been killed in a car crash on her way to work before Tony was born.

They arrive at the school and join the group of other mums and children meeting and talking in the playground before the day starts. Another car draws up, driven by the wife of a teacher – but he teaches in the large Public school twenty miles distant. They cannot afford to send their two children to the Preparatory school but there will be special terms for them to attend the Big school and there is the hope that they will gain bursaries. Meanwhile, the village school provides a standard of education for their young children which measures up to their expectations. There are only 36 pupils and two qualified teachers – a reasonable teacher/pupil ratio, although at the Prep. School the ratio is 1/5 for the younger pupils. Still, the village school has maintained a good reputation over a number of years and the teacher's wife is one of the school managers.

It is a Church school, built in 1820; old-fashioned compared with the glass and concrete structures in towns and cities. But the building is adequate and functional and provides the basic requirements of SPACE LIGHT & WARMTH for the children aged 5-11 years who begin their formal education during those early impressionable years. The large schoolroom – 100ft x 50ft – and a smaller adjoining room provide plenty of space. There are windows above head height of the children all along the south side of the building and higher windows on the east and west walls which give plenty of light. There is no central heating but two large coke-burning tortoise stoves, one at each end, provide centres of warmth on the coldest days. The smaller room is used as required for craftwork, recording, drama, play activities and the old dining tables, lino-covered, make excellent work surfaces.

School dinners (now referred to as 'lunches' after discussion with pupils and anyone interested!) are now served in the main schoolroom. Flat-topped desks are grouped together and covered with plastic tablecloths to simulate the atmosphere of a restaurant. There are tapes to be chosen and played on the cassette player bought from school funds. Teachers eat with the pupils and breaks in the timetable are just variations of activities in the ongoing programmes of work during the school day.

Marion and Tony join the small group of mothers and a few children still lingering in the playground. Suddenly Tony is shy; he has a slight stammer and does not answer Tanya, a girl who also lives in the Row and who has come to take him into school. He clutches Marion's leg, then sees Janet with her mother. The two mums are Janet who has just arrived friends and Tony and Janet often play together. It's Janet's first day as well. They have been into the school several times, for school concerts and other occasions; and, during the summer term Tony, Janet and Leslie had spent an hour on Friday afternoons with the small group of 5-6 year olds to join in whatever activity with which the group was involved – all very informal and familiar. But last term seems very distant in young Tony's memory; the present is still intimidating. Janet seems to be more confident and she takes Tanya's hand. Mrs Martin, one of the teachers whom he knows and who wears pretty glasses comes out to speak briefly to the mothers.

'Come along Tony,' she says cheerfully. 'See you soon Mrs Barnes,' she continues firmly as she takes Tony's free hand and gently removes the other which still holds on to Marion's trouser leg. But Janet an0d Tanya are there as well and soon they are all looking for Tony's and Janet's pegs in the small cloakroom. There's the picture of a dinosaur under Tony's peg and one of a rabbit under Janet's.

Soon they are sitting on mats and clapping to a tune played by the teacher on a keyboard – also bought from school funds. Tony does not even realise that his mum is not there and when he does look round for her there's only a momentary sense of her loss. The teacher has noticed the look and easily diverts his attention away from the moment of apprehension.

The first days pass easily and Mrs Martin notes that Tony does not stammer when he sings. She is confident that in time it will disappear. A future of possibilities stretches ahead.

Tony and Janet and Leslie start on their initiation into learning the skills required for their education. It's an ongoing process of learning which leads into avenues of inquiry and achievement. There are pitfalls and difficulties along the way but with the continuity of contact with the teachers through those early years the problems are recognised and help is available. Fear and anxiety are the greatest inhibitors to learning. In a village school situation it is likely that the cause of a child's distress is known to the teacher so that allowances can be made.

Janet's mother wants her to have piano lessons and the peripatetic music teacher who spends an hour a week at the school has agreed to give her a weekly lesson after school for which she will pay. The teacher has several other pupils and comes to the village on Saturday mornings to accommodate them all. Charlie, a retired postman comes into school on Friday afternoons to teach the craft of basket-making and Kate, a local artist whose son is a pupil, often comes to demonstrate, give ideas and help with the creative art work in school. The two teachers welcome all those willing and able to enrich the cultural activities of the children.

The school is a community in the larger community of the village and, as in any group of individuals who live and work together, the moral imperative cannot be ignored. Attitudes and standards are implicit in the social ethos of the school. Disruptive behaviour, bullying, absenteeism evident in the large primary schools barely exists in a situation where each child is known and knows that he/she is known.

Marion knows that Tony will have every advantage to achieve the best of which he is capable before he is faced with the challenges of examinations and further education.

The thumbnail sketches of Gary and Tony on their first days at school, one in a typical town school of 200 pupils and 7 teachers (1 being the Headteacher), the other in a village school with 2 teachers, are to demonstrate the following fundamental principles relative to the learning achievements of young children during their first 5-6 years in the state system of education.

***

1. A self-evident truth that young children learn more

212

readily and more easily in a 1/1 relationship with the teacher has been proved conclusively – and scientifically! – by the Tennessee Research project recently undertaken in America.

Speech, basic to the acquirement of reading and writing skills depends upon this relationship – especially in the more 'deprived' areas.

NB. In the Independent Schools the average ratio of teacher to young child is 1/5.

2. A child who is frightened, unhappy, anxious, does not respond to formal tuition. Transition from home to school, from parent to teacher, is difficult enough for a young child in a reasonably familiar situation; traumatic for a child who is one of 30+ others in a strange environment and separated from known surroundings. Adjustments for many take time and 'learning' is so inhibited that remedies are only partially effective – and 'falling behind' cumulative as the child moves from class to class.

Do those who measure 'standards' at the ages of 7 years and 11 years make comparisons with children such as Gary and Tony?

3. The village school – Its advantages for the young children.

Flexibility of time and space for individual children to progress at their own speed – problems and difficulties easily recognised and remedied – adaptability in response to events and circumstance.

Continuity of learning programmes in the stable teacher/child relationship.

Stability of a small community with shared interests, values and expectations – known and supported by the families it serves.

4. Buildings – expensive structures unnecessary – large institutions create their own problems! and are fixtures when the need for them no longer exists. Small schools for young children can be constructed cheaply and easily in the areas where they are required. SPACE LIGHT WARMTH TOILETS etc., are the only basic requirements.

5. Teachers – Those who choose to teach in a small school are those who understand and recognise the advantages of such a

213

situation for teaching as well as the obvious benefits for the children and the community.

(Bad teachers?? They should have been weeded out at College level!)

6. Economics – The 'village' school is economical in terms of heating and maintenance. Parental involvement with their school ensures financial support for growing needs of equipment etc.

Policy recommended:

Break down the large institutional structures for the education of young children into small, manageable units.

(I have refrained from commenting on the obvious problems relating to discipline and authority with later probable correlation to crime in the society...)

Spend money on the provision of teachers rather than on expensive buildings.

Comparisons with schools in the Independent Sector to be made at all times!

Greater use of peripatetic teachers to supplement and complement instruction in the ever-developing specialised areas of knowledge – for example, in Technology, Communication skills, Maths, Literature – or whatever is required for individual schools.

"Village Children" by Emma Smith.
A Soviet Experience.

This book was given to me by a friend who had found it in a second hand bookshop. She recognized the name of the author as the same who also had written "Maidens' Trip" an account of her experience of working on canal boats during the war, and thought I might be interested. I remembered Emma as an extremely capable boatwoman and had a very brief contact with her after the war when she lived in Putney.

"Village Children" was published – in English – in 1982 in

the U.S.S.R. after Emma had "asked to be allowed to have a look at the lives of Soviet country children... hoping really to learn something about socialism itself; not about theoretical but about practicing socialism about which I'd had no experience."

Unknowingly I followed in her footsteps in 1992 for the same reason!

The following extracts from her book are worth recording as the observations so often concur with my own ideas about the School in the community.

"School, here I began to realize, had a different meaning, and according to that different meaning it was never done; nor did any of a child's life lie outside, for simple reason that there wasn't a separate outside. In the Soviet meaning School had no boundaries to confine it but was integrated with the whole of a child's life. It had connections moreover, that travelled out like the spokes of a wheel and entered deep in the lives of the surrounding community. Between School and parents, school and the farm, school and the hospital, school and the library, school and all cultural activities, there existed a vigorous inter – relationship. And observing this I began to grasp the reality of a further fact: that in a truly socialist society it's impossible to view one aspect without reference to every other aspect. Everything is inter – related."

I am again reminded of A.N. Whitehead, our own philosopher and educator, in his continuous reference to "the seamless robe of knowledge."

The Teachers

"Increasingly I realized that no profession is thought of as being more important or is regarded more highly than teaching: it's considered an unsurpassably honourable choice of career. Teachers are expected to be, beyond question, dedicated and selfless; and certainly the ones that I encountered impressed me as being so. The positions of authority outside teaching which

Teachers occupy is evidence both of the esteem in which the profession is held and the caliber of the Teachers themselves. Again and again I met members of Local and District regional Soviets who were by profession Teachers – were people, that's to say, counted as being outstanding for their keenness of mind and their strong sense of duty. Teachers are profoundly respected by everyone; they earn the respect."

I am reminded of lines written by the poet Oliver Goldsmith in the eighteenth century. In this poem "The deserted Village" he describes the Village Schoolmaster as follows:

> While words of learned length and thundering sound,
> Amazed the gazing rustics ranged around,
> And still they gazed, and still the wonder grew
> That one small head could carry all he knew."
> Another age... but what have we lost along the way?
> Letters.

Speech

In actual fact *speech* already has been acquired by children at the age of five when they come to school; and it is on this skill, however imperfectly developed and used, that further skills to recognise such sounds represented by the written symbols are based.

Reading Schemes continue to proliferate – and no doubt they are good money-spinners for the many impoverished teachers who write them – but, at least initially, the written symbols should relate to the actual vocabulary and speech of the children themselves. The 'Janet and John' series were so popular because they reflected the speech and activities of the suburban children in the towns and cities. A very old-fashioned and almost obsolete scheme based on the character of 'Old Lob' – an old countryman – was better suited to the language and experience of the country children of Dorset.

But, a book, however simplified and colourful, can still be off-putting for a young child and, associated with the teacher's expectation of him to 'read' its contents, may well delay or even prohibit early attempts to decipher and written symbols of language. This is especially true for the less able child and for those who come from homes where there are few books and where parents are more concerned with practicalities rather than with reading to their children. Reading Schemes are useful additional aids to reading at a stage when confidence is being able to read is growing but a 'book', however limited in content and supplemented by illustrations, still remains a daunting object for most young children.

***

(Observation) I often think how much we take for granted that

217

all literate adults inevitably read books for enjoyment as well as for information. Even now, after a lifetime of reading and knowing the pleasure which most books – of my choice! – afford, to start on a 'new' (unknown to me except possibly through recommendation) author or a 'new' genre still presents me with a challenge and there's a small thrill of anticipation before I launch myself into its pages. 'Getting into a book' means that the initial hurdle of actually reading and making sense of those first pages has been passed. For example, Could I ever 'get into' a book on wargames? – unlikely!

The *'Look and Say'* method in the early stages of learning to read pre-supposes a reasonable ability to articulate words and phrases within the scope of a 5 year olds experience. (Little sense to base flash cards upon a vocabulary with which he is not familiar; content and extent of vocabulary will vary according to parental levels of interest and communication and to the geo/physical environment of home and school – although certain core words and phrases common to all, for example, bed, cat, tea, I run, you come with me, etc.)

Slurred vowels, local corruptions and idiosyncrasies of speech (thick there gaite = that gate) need to be modified and gradually corrected if the written symbol is to be equated with the spoken word as language and its usage becomes more central to all scholastic learning.

The phonetic method of learning to read can only be introduced when a child has learned to differentiate between sounds to which he has been accustomed and sounds to which he has been introduced by the teacher and which relate consistently to the written symbols which he is expected to recognise and – eventually – to reproduce in his own writing.

In 1958 I went to a course on the Pitman's *initial teaching alphabet* which claimed to facilitate the learning to read programme. It was based entirely upon phonetics and with an alphabet of six extra symbols to represent dipthongs and the undifferentiated 'ugh' sound (as in love). The lecturer referred throughout to 'buks' whereas I would have said 'boeks' and yet another might have said 'books' (as in 'troops'). I resisted the invitation to join a pilot scheme to launch the i.t.a. as it became known despite the lure of new books and materials and the prospect of visits and visitors to the school.

There is no quick and easy way for most young children learning to read and for those children who came from isolated farming communities in the west of Dorset speech was a first imperative.

A well-intentioned parent struggling financially to send two children to a private school told me that she'd not send them to the village school as their speech would be adversely affected. The comment further confirmed my own conviction that clear diction was an important basis for the acquisition of reading and writing skills.

There was an admix of social background in those 19 children and, although many came from isolated farms, the war had brought evacuees and land workers from Southampton and Portsmouth who had married and continued to live in the area. The speech of the children from these families differed in varying degrees from the speech of the local children. There were also children from two families where clear, uninflected speech was the norm (and which was *not* in any way affected by association with the Dorset dialect over the years!) and the difference in accent and clarity provided useful examples to arouse a more conscious awareness of speech and language usage in the older children.

There was no intention to abolish the local accent – even had that been possible – but only to extremes of pronunciation and to widen the limited vocabulary. In fact the poetry of W. Barnes and T. Hardy was read by all the children as near to the vernacular as possible.

Encouragement to use speech and to be aware of its relevance to reading and writing was paramount in my work with the younger children from their first days in school. There was plenty of *space* naturally. The tape recorder, which was one of the first acquisitions bought from the school fund, was kept in the smaller 'dining' room so that recording and playback was separated from the ongoing work in the main classroom. In fact 'dining' room very soon became changed to 'work' room and our dining area was moved into the main room. (more in School as a Community).

To listen, to experiment with sounds as in other languages, to exercise the physical muscular use of lips and tongue, to know about breathing and the mechanics of producing variations of voice were all integral to the programmes I devised for these children. Singing, dancing, acting and most other activities centred upon this cultivation of language. I introduced them to simple colloquial phrases in French used in a repetitive mimicry of the sounds unrelated to the written word so that, 'ouvrez la porte', 'comment ca va?' etc. became easy alternatives in which to exercise their skills. We also sang 'Sur le pont d'Avignon' etc. and a 'pop' song at the time 'Que sera, sera' provided an additional stimulus to experiment with sounds and words in other languages. Recently, a one-time pupil of the school reminded me that they had sung a song in German about a huntsman and she could still remember the line, 'ich bin ein jagersman'!

Speech and Reading and Writing (however clumsy and badly formed) are skills basic to most further learning and are not acquired in isolation but in association with all the ongoing activities and learning programmes throughout the years in primary school and beyond. With all and every method I could devise I would get those children speaking, reading and writing each according to his/her ability and stage of development in experience and understanding.

More importantly I hoped to instil a regenerative interest and love of literature.

Books, for many young children, who may not come from homes where parents themselves read acquire and value books, are intimidating. Climbing the stairs at an earlier stage of development presented a similar hurdle but with an obvious incentive to make the necessary effort. The incentive to learn how to read a book is not so obvious! *Motivation* is all as most teachers know.

Making one's own book, however simple, using familiar words and situations and adding decorations of one's own initiative is as good an introduction to this world of books with which a young child can cope. Books can be made so easily; just the basic ingredients of paper and all the variety of objects which make marks on the paper are necessary. And paper is so easily available – paper of varying textures, colours and shapes detract from the threat implicit in the conventional format of the books being read by older children. Even the shape of one's own book could be different – large or small, shaped like a concertina to stand on a ledge, loose-leaved tied with – anything! – to be re-arranged, reduced or supplemented as required, and 'books' as varied in format and content as the children are able to devise.

With only 19 children there was always the possibility of co-operation with an older child to add his/her expertise to the earlier efforts in his own learning programmes – the teacher always aware and in control of the situation.

Books are so exciting – or at least they ought to be! And for children good stories, good illustrations, clear print and durable covers help them to realise that an half-hour's read can be as exciting as knocking out the monster on the video screen – more imaginative, less repetitive! It was always an occasion during the autumn term when the orders for new books and equipment arrived. We'd have a wonderful day exploring the piles of new books, pristine and still smelling 'like wood shavings' as one boy once said. I, or one of the older children would read an interesting or exciting extract to give the 'flavour' of a book's content. Everyone was involved in various ways at getting to know what was available in this latest addition to our library. Learning to care for the books so that we could always buy new ones instead of replacements was an imperative from that day when a 5 year old was introduced to a 'proper' book which he might handle and look at to the avid reader who often forgot about thumb marks and the frailty of a book's spine. (I think particularly of Shaun who read through my three volumes of Tolkein's 'Lord of the Rings' which I had taken into school in order to read a certain extract; and he was 10 years old!)

Books at every level of ability for enjoyment and reference were on order.

Some excellent writers for children were being published: Leon Garfield, H Treece, Mary Norton, Rosemary Sutcliffe were among those I remember. But also I introduced suitable excerpts from my own reading. I hope that the names of Laurence Durrell, Gavin Maxwell, Tolkein, Desmond Morris et al. are still recognised by those to whom I introduced my own love of good literature.

The Curriculum

During that first term there were four evenings each week when I could concentrate on formulating programmes of work for individual children and also for group work to cover the frameworks of subject content based on a five year plan. This would avoid repetition, I hoped ('please Miss, we did the Vikings last year') although I knew that demarcation lines of subject content were often deceptive and misleading. However, initially a framework for work schedules was necessary in order to get us launched into more flexible and interest-generated schemes. Centres of interest and project work were a natural development of how we worked as the subject demarcation lines became blurred and fused. But my early schemes were subject based and included the usual range of subjects taught in primary schools at the time: Scripture, English (reading and writing), Arithmetic, History, Geography, Nature Study (optional), Singing, Physical Training, Drawing, Needlework (for the girls!) and Woodwork (for the boys) if materials were available. The content of each subject area depended upon the knowledge and interest of the individual teachers. There were set text books – dull, limited and uninspiring – on which to base syllabus content.

The framework for such clearly defined subjects to be taught had been established by the time that I had entered my two years' training in a London college in 1932. Most of the training was concerned with what to teach and the materials (books) and methods necessary to ensure an efficient teaching system. With classes of 30-40 children confined in a limited space most teaching was based upon 'chalk and talk', the lesson content recapitulated by the children in the form of written exercises and/or verbal question-and-answer testing.

From the age of 7 years onwards this instruction depended

upon the ability level of the children to read, the inference being that the basic skill had been acquired in the Infants' school. It must be obvious that many children left school at the statuary age of 14 years barely literate.

Maths was reduced to *Arithmetic* with pages of sums reflecting an ability – or lack of it – to compute the four rules in number, money, length, weight and capacity with little or no reference to any form of practical application. It consisted of a series of tricks by which to manipulate the numbers involved, for example, two ways to subtract 268 from 537, two (or more?) ways of doing long division and quick methods of computing 4 pairs of socks at 1.11¾ (shillings and pence!) a pair. A daily 10 minutes stint of mental Arithmetic, written or verbal, was deemed to be essential. Calculators, computers and decimalisation belonged to the real of science/fiction – also unheard of!

My early attitude attempts, twenty years later, to formulate work programmes for those 19 children were based upon a framework of those subjects in which I myself had been educated and trained to teach. In that first village school where I had charge of the juniors the Headmaster had provided me with the syllabus which covered the content of the subjects I was to teach. I was also provided with a Record book, returned to him each Friday afternoon for him to initial the entries of what I had taught in each subject. Good training, I'm sure, in the habit of keeping records of work on a regular basis, although my own forecasts and records of work programmes were more detailed and often changed and re-written as the needs arose.

The use of language in all its forms was always dominant in my list of priorities; its cultivation and development was inherent in all and every 'subject' and activity.

'The ogre does what ogres can,
Deeds quite impossible for man.
But one prize is beyond his reach,
The ogre cannot master speech.
Across a subjugated plain,
Among its desperate and slain,
The ogre strolls with hands on hips,

223

While drivel gushes from his lips.'
W H Auden

And, for me, Auden says it all!

A Teachers' Centre was established in a nearby town where teachers and advisors could meet to discuss and disseminate ideas and information. It was also a resource centre where apparatus, books and equipment could be examined and even borrowed. An enthusiastic and knowledgeable Headteacher set up a Maths workshop in his school where teachers were invited to participate in devising work cards and programmes suitable for their own pupils.

Schools of Education attached to the Universities offered courses to help teachers re-assess and re-vitalise all aspects of teaching at primary level. I was to avail myself of a year's study at the Bristol School in 1965 (at the expense of Dorset Local Education Authority) and it was a most stimulating year of interest and enlightenment – a year which should be readily available to all teachers at a suitable phase in their careers.

Help was necessary during that period of an expanding curriculum and with the thrust of ideas and theories related to the education of young children; and help was available for those teachers willing and enthusiastic enough to take advantage of the opportunities on offer.

I look back and see the band-wagons of ideas, opinions and theories trundling through the established routines and practices of classroom teaching. But band-wagons have a tendency to take over and to suppress the more formal and established practices. I remember being alerted to the 'band-wagon syndrome' one day when I was busy with a group of pupils making an effort to correct common mis-spellings of words such as 'here, hear; bare, bear; etc.' The standard practice was to put each work into a sentence to indicate its meaning. Then further sentences were written by each child to ensure that spellings and meanings were understood. As I was demonstrating on the blackboard, the door opened and our HMI stood there. The visits were always unpredictable and without warning. I was 'caught out' and felt guilty! His words further emphasised my unease: 'I never thought to see you teaching in such a way,' he said; and I was suitably mortified.

At a later date I would have justified my reason for such an exercise but the authority of an HMI was absolute to a primary school teacher. I think of Hardy's schoolteacher heroine in 'Under the Greenwood Tree' who fainted when suddenly she became aware that the Inspector was in the room; and this account was no exaggeration of the effect that such a visit could induce. At the time, project work, creative writing, free expression and learning through experiment and research were the slogans and any form of class teaching was regarded as retrospective. Most teachers know that there is time and place for both formal and informal methods of teaching the basic skills of literacy and numeracy. I had no firm antagonism to the repetitive litany of tables chanted on a daily basis by a whole class of children except that it was boring and took up too much time.

I imagine that the current slogan of 'back to basics' finds favour with many who base opinions on their own limited experience of 'schooling'. Such a slogan would have supported my own occasional retreat into formal instruction and exercise methods of teaching and would have justified my 'lapse' to the visiting Inspector. But Inspectors, Advisors and teachers alike were carried along by the impetus of successive band-wagons in those post-war years, so often with a disregard for all that had been achieved previously (even though they themselves were products of past schooling and education). Rational appraisal and analysis of educational theories was still limited, later to be more widely practised and disseminated through the extended degree courses for teachers by educationalists such as Professors Hirst, Peters, Flew, Wilson et.al.

The curriculum has been under constant revision and expansion during the past forty years. The age of technology has posed yet more problems for educationalists. Simple teaching machines and calculators already were in use during my years in Whitechurch. We had a TV in the house and a group of pupils watched the Science programmes devised by Gerd Sommerhof. They were excellent, with follow-up suggestions for further work in the classroom which supplemented my own limited

225

knowledge in this area. I welcomed these additional aids to my teaching programmes but wonder how I would have acquired the many skills and information now required to initiate young children into the discriminatory usage of such a range of technological aids to learning and communication. The introduction of the *National Curriculum* to provide guidelines through this ever expanding universe of knowledge and methodology must have been a welcome support for most teachers.

A re-vitalising of the content and understanding of the different subject areas was instigated by an enthusiastic Education Officer (the same who had voted for my appointment!). Courses organised by specialists in their fields, proliferated and most were excellent and well attended by teachers in each locality. Miss Biggs revolutionised and enhanced my limited understanding of *Mathematics*.

Instead of 'arithmetic' which consisted of exercises with numbers and measurements which had little or no connections with the concrete realities they represented. I was introduced to an understanding of mathematical concepts with language such as symmetry, equality, balance, estimations, radius, etc. which fleshed out the arid tricks represented by pages of sums.

We weighed and measured, we estimated lengths and distances and costed provisions from catalogues – and indulged in a whole range of activities devised by the experts to encourage our understanding of mathematical concepts as well as developing our skills to manipulate numbers.

Experimentation, assessment, correction and careful recording of procedures and results depended heavily upon the children's use of speech, reading and writing.

A. N. Whitehead's references to the 'seamless robe of knowledge' became increasingly evident. *Jean Piaget's* research into the psychology of learning, particularly relevant to young children, was being reported in articles of Educational journals and magazines. My own limited understanding that pages of sums, learning tables by rote were just tricks to be learnt and remembered as abstractions unrelated to any specific function gradually clarified as I read some of the articles. The key phase for children of primary school age was *concrete operational* and all meaningful learning for them should be based on what they can directly experience. Miss Biggs and our efforts to weigh and measure etc. etc. were justified by the results of Piaget's observational research work with young children.

In 1958 a *Dr Gattegno* from Italy, came to Bridport to introduce usage of *Cuisenaire Rods* to aid children in their understanding of numeracy. The wooden rods were related to size, colour and number – for example – a white cube measuring one cubic centimetre represents the unit of *one*, a green cube measuring 2 centimetres, *two* and so on to the ten cubic centimetre cube which was coloured light brown. The rods were packed neatly into a compartmentalised box. They were pleasing to look at, well finished and smooth to the touch. The children found them easy to use and manipulate – so easy to *see* that 2 fives make 10! Cubic capacity as well as length was self-evident when demonstrated with their use. Relative size and inversions (2 x 5 = 10 and 5 x 2 = 10) were soon recognised and I found the use of the rods invaluable especially with the younger children in the early stages of their number work.

I leaned heavily on books in which programmes of work with children were based on these more recent developments in the teaching of Maths and a series written by the team of Flavell and Wakelham was of great help and support as so often I was learning alongside the children.

The separated subjects of Arithmetic, Algebra and Geometry – and later another mystery called Trigonometry – had formed the basis of my own youthful introduction to Mathematics and which I dismissed from my studies as soon the essential examination had been passed. As I listened and learned from Miss Biggs during those evening sessions in Bridport I began to understand that the language of Mathematics was as exciting as the language of the poets and the philosophers; at so many levels they were interchangeable.

All the subject areas were under constant review and reappraisal with suggestions and recommendations for more enlightened ways of introducing young children to the wealth of knowledge and experience which was their cultural heritage.

History no longer consisted of stories such as Alfred and the cakes, Alexander and his horse Bucephalus or even Henry

227

8th and his various wives. Lists of monarchs and the dates of their reigns were just lists of names and figures to young children unrelated to anyone or anything within their experience. History must start with the children themselves, their families, the village, town and locality where they lived. Museums, local records, letters and documents would be examined to interpret and clarify past events – gradually to lead out from the known centre of their own local history to the wider scene of events and movements. I had to do my own research and moved into the disciplines of archaeology, architecture and other 'ologies' as well!

History 'stories' still continued with the younger children along with Jack and the Beanstalk & Billy Goat Gruff! At least names such as Hereward the Wake, Alexander the Great, Prince Charlie, et al. would be familiar landmarks in later studies of historical events and, as I had always loved stories from whatever source during my own youthful years in an Infants' school, I presumed that the younger children – and often some of the less able – would also enjoy stories being told or read to them. The art of storytelling with mime and gesture was also introduced and practised by older children when the opportunities arose. (Continual use of speech!) This all tied up with the formal and informal drama sessions, with the making of a puppet theatre, with dance and movement, with singing and music making; in fact with all of our ongoing learning activities at different times.

With only 19 children and plenty of space the rigid timetable which I had carefully prepared before the term started soon became ignored. The only fixed period of time was from 9 am until 9.5 am for the obligatory morning assembly and Religious Instruction but even this tended to meld into other areas of our work schemes. (Stories again!)

The gift of imagination with its concomitant talent for lateral thinking was often a threat to a more disciplined schedule of learning; there were always so many tangents of interesting possibilities to lead further into our voyages of discovery. There was need continually to exercise a strong effort of will to keep a balance between the separate disciplines of learning and to ensure that progress for each and every child was monitored and recorded. This requirement put a grid and a limit to my own flights of fancy.

So that we were all aware of the directions which we pursued as the centres of interest developed from incidental enthusiasms we kept flow charts of all the topics and work in which groups and individuals became involved. Sometimes these diagrammatic records were simple and of short-lived duration. Others expanded as new information and suggestions were added. The diagrams were large, often drawn on a roll of wallpaper (I was good at 'scrounging' from helpful shopkeepers) with charcoal or those ubiquitous greasy crayons, and either displayed (if tidy enough!) or available (between covers) for reference and consultation.

I remember one such centre of interest when Pat brought in a dried snake's skin which had been sloughed off in a nearby gravel pit. I wish I had kept some of those diagrams which would have shown how schemes of work were initiated from a patterned and paper skin of a field snake, a couch shell brought back by a friend from a visit to Egypt – driftwood collected from the beach in Charmouth.

Geography

I asked the older children what work they had been doing in Geography.

'Maps,' I was told and Sylvia produced a dog-eared sheet of paper on which was cyclostyled (the word is now obsolete, succeeded by photo-copying) a map of the world.

'We had to write in all the capitals of different countries,' she told me.

'We drew in all the big rivers,' added someone else.

I had in fact found a whole heap of these maps copied from an old atlas and had consigned them to the rubbish pile along with the worm-eaten cupboard in which I had found them.

Geography was still timetabled on my early schedules of work for two ½ hourly periods each week.

As with History, we started from base. Local names of farms and fields, possible derivations. ('Cold Comfort Farm' and 'Animal Farm' linked up with books borrowed from the travelling library...)

The Church and the War Memorial (1914-1918 were focal

points in the village and provided plenty of historical and geographical material for investigation and recording.

The younger children joined in our forays to the Church and to the nearby stream where we looked for otter marks and the occasional amonite still to be found as relics from a distant past when the low-lying river bed had been under the sea.

Charmouth – the blue lias clay – amonites and geologists with their hammers were on our doorstep.

Hardown and Pilsden – Saxon earthworks – flints and arrow-heads in a small local Museum were all within visiting distance and we took full advantage of a directive from the Local Education Authority encouraging teachers to move out from the confines of the classroom to visit places of local interest. I began to enlist the aid of one or two mothers on such excursions to be with the younger children while I directed the older ones to the more serious purpose of our 'outings'.

Preparation and recordings were all-important aspects of our visits to justify our 'meanderings' to parents, Managers and the odd Inspector who occasionally called unannounced. (After one such unannounced visit when he had found the school empty I was required to inform the 'Office' of my proposed outings at least two weeks in advance – difficult to predict weather conditions so far ahead!)

It soon became obvious that the subject divisions between History and Geography became blurred and irrelevant. My own plans and records of work and projects became identified as 'Local Studies'. Gradually, individual children developed specific interests and then I worked on the Dalton plan where individual schemes of suggestions and work were prepared as and when necessary. But, in that first term when I was finding out what was known – not known – and how best to devise stratagems of work to stimulate interest and effort much of our day-to-day 'lessons' were participated by all at their varying levels of ability.

Felicity and Sylvia and Kay in the 'top' group were most helpful during those early days as I began to sort out learning difficulties which would need to be remedied for one or two children in the 'middle' group. (Judith was allowed to join in wherever the fancy took her!)

Harry and Vernon, the two senior boys, also did their share; in charge of the games and PE equipment and keeping the stoves well stoked when it was cold!

In 1987, Sylvia was to publish her own study of traditional occupations, customs and activities of the Marshwood Vale, fast disappearing in a period of radical changes to the established rural community.

'Dorset's Western Vale' – Sylvia Creed.

Published 1987 – Dorset Publishing Co. Milborne Port.

Music

I was no 'musician' but I could play the piano for hymn singing and for Country Dancing (I was also committed to taking the Church Choir – more anon.) and I also learned how to make and to play recorder-type pipes from bamboo. I was always convinced that all forms of Musical activity were integral with the core subjects of the curriculum.

I recently heard a programme in which Evelyn Glennie spoke of her own experience as a totally deaf musician. (She is world famous as a percussion virtuoso.) When the tonal quality and timbre of her speaking voice was commented upon she said that it was due to her training as a musician. I think of Helen Keller, deaf and blind from birth who was able to learn and understand speech and language through other sensory experience and training.

All the physical exercises necessary for singing, for rhythmic movement and dance contribute to the enunciation of clear speech, reinforce awareness of the power and variety of tone and pitch in the use of the voice.

It was always good to hear children sing either in the formal context of a lesson, rehearsing for a Spring concert or humming when otherwise occupied... We were very good on hymns!

The Assistant Officer for Education, keen to improve the standards of education, especially in the small rural schools, appointed Advisors to encourage and give new impetus to the old established methods and content of their specialist subject areas.

I recall one memorable occasion when over a hundred teachers had been persuaded to attend a day's course on the teaching of music. It was held in a cold, dreary hall with rows of utility chairs as the only furniture. Transport to Dorchester from the more distant corners of the county was not easy – few teachers had cars, fewer still had phones to make the necessary arrangements. We had given up a precious Saturday to attend the course and Music was not considered to be of great importance in the curriculum – one of the 'frills'. We were a group of cynical and reluctant teachers, each one ready to abscond for a more profitable dash around the shops when the opportunity arose.

It was a daunting situation for the youthful enthusiast who was introduced to us as a 'musician eager to promote musical experience for all in the schools'.

We sat, stoically cold and sceptical, wondering if coffee would be provided. From the first moments when she told us to put the chairs around the sides of the room, we were captivated. Her voice was warm and clear, authoritative and yet persuasive; a musical voice. I was even more convinced during that first hour that the cultivation of voice and speech was dominant in the related skills of reading and writing. Her confidence and enthusiasm dispelled all thoughts of truanting. She fed us with ideas, teaching us as we might teach the children in our schools.

She introduced us to chime bars and the pentatonic scale on which we could devise tunes which always harmonise. We worked in groups, improvising percussion effects and rhythms on a selection of miscellaneous objects she had located on a trestle table. From a random cacophony of sounds in various parts of the hall she assembled and organised a simple and repetitive 'orchestral' piece. We were as motivated to 'get it right' as any group of young children might be!

Coffee was indeed provided although there was little enough time to indulge in a coffee break. Even after an hour's break for lunch, everyone was ready and waiting for the afternoon session to begin. We were all involved throughout the varied and stimulating programme the young musician had organised for us. (She was not so young, we discovered; mid thirties and had been a flautist in the National Youth Orchestra.)

We sang, we hummed, we whistled, we clapped and tapped with feet and fingers.

And we listened.

We listened to recordings of 'mood' music, dance music, music for accompanying choral speaking and, no doubt, much more.

At the end as we drank tea, the musician (and I regret that her name eludes me) played 'The Gollywogs Cakewalk' on her flute for us. She must have been exhausted but also heartened by the roar of applause she received from the group of teachers, also tired but now animated and convinced that music making was of the utmost importance for all aspects of development in young children.

Chime bars, a glockenspiel, a xylophone and drums were noted for inclusion on my next requisition order.

That one day in Dorchester had lifted my own appreciation and sensitivity to music in all its variety of expression and performance and no longer was it a 'subject' relegated to a timetabled half hour on one afternoon a week. It was yet another integral part of this 'seamless robe of knowledge'.

Discipline

I was no disciplinarian.

Strong vocal chords backed up by equally strong determination and output of will-power to coerce, impel, motivate, inspire even reluctant pupils to sit still, listen and regurgitate half-digested facts and exercises and notions alien to their own immediate experience and interests were attributes better suited to the barrack room than to the classroom.

As a pupil myself, I had enjoyed learning, had been more than anxious to please my teachers whom I aspired to emulate. Entry to the Girls' Grammar School in the mid-twenties was restricted to those whose aspirations and achievements were based upon a love of learning for its own sake as well as for its more practical value in terms of vocation and employment. We were an elite who valued our initiation into a wealth of recorded experience and ideas. Failure to fulfill the expectations of teachers resulted in an unobtrusive withdrawal from the school long before pupil failure became identified and emphasised through the national examination system.

Continuation of this rarefied scholastic education continued until I was almost nineteen years old when I gained entrance to a Teacher Training College in London – the peak of ambition for such as myself. Latin at Matriculation level was required for entry to a University and Latin was not included in the curriculum of our small school. There were only 120 pupils with a staff of 7, most of whom were required to teach a subject in addition to their own specialism – (the Games mistress taught Scripture; Science and Geography, were similarly 'bonded'.) The staff/pupil ratio was more than generous but choices in the spread of subjects on the curriculum had to be made and the Headmistress wisely decided to include Needlework and

Domestic Science in preference to Latin. Possible candidates for entry to University from such a school were extremely rare; I only remember two who achieved such distinction; both only children whose parents were able to afford private tuition in Latin and the considerable cost of a 3 year course at a University.

I was more than fortunate to be considered for a place in a T T College and more than fortunate to be funded by an interest free loan from a Girls' Career Association, the loan to be repaid, in full and with an additional donation to help others like myself during the first three years of my career. I was a girl after all and with two younger brothers. My father, himself an orphan brought up in a London orphanage, was struggling to make a living as a self-employed hairdresser – the trade to which he had been apprenticed early in the 1900s. My mother filled the spare bedrooms in the rambling 3 storey house (freezing in winter with only a coal fire in the living room for heating!) with lodgers to remedy the shortfall of income. (Really she enjoyed the company – and she was a good cook!) It was a pity that I was not the daughter she deserved and our relationship was so much at odds – for both of us. But she supported my obsession for a teaching career; she'd have been a good teacher herself, given the chance... My father was a studious man who loved reading. His interests were focused on the Church Lads' Brigade which he ran for thirty years giving instruction in band Music, in Physical Training and in Bible Study for three evenings a week and every Sunday afternoon. (Voluntary and unpaid!) He was also a staunch supporter of the Mission Church founded and conducted by my Mother's uncle – a lay preacher and at the bottom of the ecclesiastical hierarchy in the Abbey town! I wish I had known him better but he was a withdrawn person to me and he died before I had reached a level of understanding which might have enabled me to bridge the gap.

My years at the Grammar school provided the perfect escape from a family situation with which I felt at odds. I spent evenings and weekends in my attic bedroom reading and studying. I lived in a world peopled by characters from the Brontes, from Hardy, Austen, Eliot and was away on my travels with R.L.S with Jeffrey Arnold, D K Broster, A P Herbert et al. I also read my parents' library books – Rider Haggard, Ethel M Dell and all the 'who dunnits' enjoyed by my father. I was in love with the poets – Shelley, Keats, Lamartine, Baudelaire, etc, etc, and with the aesthetic inaccessibility of a curate or two!

The two years at College further immersed me in the world of literature. I took advanced courses in French and English with Music and Weaving as subsiduaries. Teaching Practices in the Secondary schools were in very controlled situations with the class teacher always present to prevent any possible disruption to the strictly timetabled lessons which I 'presented' to the forty or more pupils.

Such lessons were prepared in term of content and method then delivered orally with an occasional visual aid (a picture, an object...) the content then regurgitated by the pupils in the form of written answers to questions from the blackboard... 'Chalk and talk'. Problems of discipline and control did not arise as only the efficient class teachers had charge of students; even the College tutors who came to supervise and report deferred to the teacher's opinion and assessment of the student in her class.

From this unlikely background of my own education and later training I was plunged into the harsh reality of controlling a class of 35 seniors (11 – 14 in a country school back in Dorset. This was a class of slow learners, most of whom were barely literate and who resented being still at school. My classroom was rigidly organised in 5 x 8 rows of desks and was separated from that of the Headmaster (who taught the brighter pupils) by a sliding glass-panelled screen so that I was always on view. Only his surveillance kept the behaviour of my class at a tolerance level as I nervously proffered the detailed preparation of each day's lessons. No doubt with the best of intentions, the Headmaster used to take over from me to demonstrate how *he* would conduct such a lesson while I watched, wretched and humiliated in front of this class of young adults who resented being the 'backward' class and resented my inability to impress and control.

The other two teachers, both 'uncertificated' (had not been to College) had no such problems. Both had classes of 40 upwards of mixed ability junior children and from both rooms emerged a steady hum of silence broken only by instructions and injunctions from the teacher.

How was it done?

I was the only teacher apart from the Headmaster who had been to College. It seemed that I had not learned the most basic essential of class control and reaffirmed in their opinions that two years spent in College training was a waste of time – the only benefit being in the difference of our wage packets!

I was overtaken by Nemesis during my second term when a whole group of the class refused to leave the classroom for the bleak playground exercises of the PE lesson.

I was reported to the Education Officer at County Hall as being incompetent.

It is barely credible that in 1937 the driving force in the Education Office was a Miss Miller whose official position was that of Chief Clerk! She came to the school, inspected all the pupils' work books, my own record book and became my ally. She told me to go sick until the end of the term and then to apply for a post to teach the juniors (7-11 years) in Gaunts village school at the far end of the county. Briefly, I took her advice and was appointed.

There were three teachers, the Headmaster who took the seniors (aged 11-14 years) myself in charge of the juniors and the uncertificated teacher (with the geese and the privy across the paddock and with whom I was to lodge) taught the youngest. There were only 60-70 pupils at any one time so that there was only an average of 20 for whom I was responsible. The one-to-one relationship between teacher and children, of central importance to the teacher/learning situation, would now be possible.

Yet my self-esteem had been severely damaged. Poor disciplinarians went to teach in the country schools where, presumably, pupils were more docile and less aware of possibilities for disruptive and rebellious attitudes to authority.

An inability to discipline senior pupils meant a demotion – for this is how such a change was regarded in the hierarchy of teacher prestige – to be in charge of younger children. (How that mis-conception has been turned on its head with studies in child psychology demonstrating the importance of those early years when foundations for most future learning are laid.)

237

I went to Gaunts school for the summer term – 1937 – with romantic and idealised notions of myself as mentor and dispenser of knowledge reduced to a more realistic acknowledgement that the basis of my teaching was to be grounded in the 3 R's organised on a daily repetitive programme of Scripture, Reading, Writing, with more Reading and Writing incorporated into simplified narratives designated as History and Geography.

Experience is not enough

'In my experience,' – even when stated with conviction is not in itself justifiable evidence to support a debatable issue. Much depends upon the nature and relevance of the experience. 'We learn through experience,' – that is to be hoped for but the value of what we learn for ourselves and those we influence depends a great deal on the depth of understanding we bring to reflect upon our experience; and this understanding does not 'like Topsy' grow of itself but develops in constant interaction with the thoughts and opinions of others.

When I decided to apply for the post of Headteacher in a village school I had both the enthusiasm and a relevant variety of experience to qualify me for a pre-selection interview with the then Deputy Education Officer who had a special interest in primary schools, having been a teacher of young children himself – unusual in those days when promotion to the Administration was hardly ever from the 'ranks'. (Sadly, he was to die prematurely from overwork.) I drove my husband's car – a large black Consul – to County Hall for the interview. I was the right age (40), was married (an advantage in the fifties after decades of stereotyped spinster teacher), I dressed well (my one well-pressed suit), I did not speak with an alien accent and had been educated at a prestigious local Grammar school. I had 'further experience'. First impressions, even at a superficial level, were important to deter opinions based on prejudice and stereotype. My 'further experience' was listed in the introductory letter I had written to express my interest in village schools.

1936-1939 – A village school. 70 pupils aged 5-14 years. Headmaster. Myself in charge of 25 juniors aged 7-11 years and with responsibility for taking Needlework and Physical Training with all the girls aged 7-14 years. The infants were in the charge of teacher in her fifties who had been at the school all her life as a pupil, then as a Monitor and eventually as a teacher.

(Our salaries were paid in cash on the last Friday each month by the school correspondent who came out from the nearest town in a taxi with the money which was ceremoniously paid to each of us from the Headmaster's desk!)

1941-1943 – Supply teaching in Oxford and London in secondary schools specialising in the teaching of English and French.

1946-1949 – British Forces Educational Services stationed in Germany. (I had taken a course in German at the Polytechnic while teaching in London.)

A colleague and myself were detailed to requisition a building and staff for a multi-racial school in Bad Salzuflen for children aged 5-13 years from the families of the Allied Missions stationed there. Under the auspices of the TOCH, I also gave lessons in English Literature to English speaking German pupils in the gymnasium (or High School) I was responsible for most of the teaching with the older pupils, and for devising a syllabus appropriate to the special requirements of such a school. (French, Szech, Yugo-Slav, Belgian all want to learn English. There were some English pupils as well!)

1952-1955 – Some supply teaching in a local Senior school. 2 years full time teaching a class of infants (5-7 years) in a nearby village school. (for which I had to learn about Reading Schemes, early Mathematics beginning to replace the limitations of Arithmetic with young children and to immerse myself in the available literature – mostly articles in the Teachers World and the Times Ed. Supplement – to know the 'how' and 'what' I should be teaching.)

My letter and the brief résumé of my experience was on the desk – in evidence! The interview was informal but thorough.

'How did I organise the work and the timetable in the multi-racial school?"

I explained that I worked largely on the Dalton Plan which involved the preparation of assignments of work (typed) for individual children on a weekly basis, the preparation of work cards in English, French and German to suggest activities and 'projects' (an up-and-coming addition to the language) which could be ongoing with minimal supervision while I was busy with small group teaching. Unifying activities such as singing, some dance-drama, excursion's to places of interest, some craftwork were also important.

'A busy life,' commented the interviewer. I agreed that it was.

'Why did you leave?'

'Marriage and children,' I replied.

'Why a run-down village school?'

'I believe that small schools provide the best environment for the more formalised education of young children. I also believe in the value of the village school to the community.'

It was necessary to curtail my enthusiasm; the man would be wary of romanticised idealism. I mentioned briefly that I was greatly influence by the writing of Karl Popper ('The Open Society – and its enemies.') and by Professor Ayer's early work on Language and Logic... Enthusiasm was not enough...

'What about the Church? You would need to be a Communicant Member.'

I assured him that I had been brought up in the traditional Church of England framework. A mental flashback to the kindly Vicar added an edge of sincerity to my answer. Doubts about the whole institutionalised nature and function of the Church were to come later. Reinforced by Bishop Robinson's 'Honest To God' debate in which I was to take some very small part.

Finally, the crucial question which I knew was uppermost in his mind could no longer be avoided. He picked up my letter of introduction as he asked; I knew that I had made no mention of my personal affairs. He had the sensitivity to be slightly embarrassed about asking but this was 1955 when married women with careers – at least in teaching – were regarded with suspicion. Eleven years later when I was being interviewed for the post of lecturer in a College of Education, I pre-empted the question by stating that I did not live with my husband and that my mongol daughter aged 16 years and my younger daughter aged 8 years lived at home with me. To my amazement the Principal – a woman! – said that such experience could only be an advantage and that a flat on the College campus would be available if I was appointed. As I was well read in the recent literature by Hirst, Peters, Dearden, Wilson, Tibble et al. concerning the philosophic approach to the study of Education the formal interview posed no problems and I was appointed. Any personal difficulties were my own affair impinging on my professional work only to the same extent that it would be for a man who, for whatever reason, had no wife.

But in 1955 the question asked by the Education Officer was the all-important one.

'What about your husband and your children?' he asked. How was he to know that I even had children, I thought. However, I had my explanation ready. My husband was a farmer who suffered badly from asthma; he would have to give up the farm whatever happened. I was sure that he would have no difficulty in finding alternative employment.

The real hurdle – for him and the Managers of the school – was going to be my mongol daughter. Any form of mental handicap was still treated with suspicion and ignorance. I had brought photos of her taken in the garden in which, although the defect was evident, she looked much like any other cheerful six-year old. I had to persuade this man that to include Judith as a pupil in the school was not only feasible but could be of value in the sensitivity, moral and social attitudes of adults as well as children in the community. Children with physical disabilities and emotionally disturbed children had to be accommodated by most teachers in the schools and should mental handicap be a separate category? It was a question of degree of course.

Judith's speech was very limited but she had been well trained in acceptable social habits. I had always been determined that she would share in all our activities as a family although with due regard to her limitations.

The I Q (Intelligence Quotient) for measuring the mental aptitude of a child was much in vogue. I said that in my present village school (where I was in charge of 25 children aged 5-7/8 years) there were two children with very low I Q's of 75 and 80 (100 being the norm) and that Judith's I Q would be only slightly lower. I was persuasive enough in my convincing argument to persuade Mr Easton that I knew that once I had the backing of authority I had a good chance of succeeding.

Giles, aged 8 years would also be a pupil in the school although, if it didn't work for either or both of us, he could to one of the two other village schools each only 3 miles distant. My husband would be able to drive him there if necessary.

It was a lengthy and exhausting interview and I had questions of my own relating to more practical considerations of the building and what money would be available for equipment and books.

Those lavatories and those desks...

I was assured, albeit reservedly, that money would be made available to meet with my requirements should I be appointed. From the Church or the Local Authority? I persisted, knowing that, generally, the secular L A schools were in better condition than their Church supported counterparts.

My enthusiasm was backed up by a realistic appraisal of the situation as it was and how I would hope to improve it, met with approval.

The value of my experience of teaching all age groups in the 5-15 years age range and in various types of schools augmented by my reading – Bantock and Dewey were among my still limited references – so that I had clarified for myself certain precepts I considered to be central for the success of myself as a teacher and for the children with whom I would work.

The central precept which determines all subsequent theories and opinions is that a school for children aged 5-11 years should be small with approximately 100 pupils.

Curriculum Assessment

Enthusiasm is not enough.

It is so easily deflated when beset by adverse criticism and one's own doubts and uncertainties. As with a doctor, a lawyer, an actor, enthusiasm for the work must be grounded in a solid – although flexible – body of knowledge relevant to the specialised nature of his work. The central core of the old two year Teacher Training course was concerned with introducing students to the programmes of methodology related to the mental, physical, social and moral growth of the young child and with providing limited experience in which to practise developing skills of introducing children to the basic skills of numeracy, literacy (reading and writing) and a limited number of subjects (at a simple level). The emphasis was on 'how' and 'what' to teach with little or no concern with 'why' this method or that; 'why' needlework for the girls, and football for the boys; 'why' religious instruction. As such, the limited body of knowledge with which a young teacher was equipped to start on a teaching career in a primary school during the thirties and forties of the twentieth century, was factual and comprehensible by the young teacher her/himself too immature to be concerned with the 'whys' and 'wherefores' of what and how the young were being taught. The timetable was strictly compartmentalised into rigidly adhered to units of time throughout the day and the curriculum was packaged by subjects into a five-yearly programme of work usually devised by the existing Headteacher. This worked reasonably well when the population served by the school was reasonably static. The young teacher was given firm guidelines in the one-year, one-class system; confidence in class management was gained and, over the period of five years in the primary school an acceptable body of skills was acquired by most pupils. Continuity and stability of teachers and work in a school often offset the possibilities for stagnation, complacency and a resistance to change inherent in such a situation.

From the late fifties onwards established social structures in towns and villages began to shift and parental mobility produced a few cracks in the established patterns of curriculum content which, despite a certain uniformity, varied according to the individual interests and rationale of the Headteacher.

'Miss, I did the Romans in my last school,' typifies a recurring difficulty facing a classroom teacher, and a bright primary school child who is bored soon loses the enthusiasm and impetus which fuels his drive to learn and to experiment. Frustration and boredom erupt into disruptive behaviour contained only by an enforced and rigid discipline.

Enthusiasm is not enough

The limited definitions of the teacher's role and the 'what' and 'how of the curriculum content and organisation in a primary school was gradually eroded by what is referred to as the 'Scientific Revolution' and the explosion of knowledge not only in the areas of Science and Technology but in the familiar subject areas as well. History, limited to 'fairy tales' from the past were obsolete. Facts had to be verified, supported by reputable evidence measurement, telling the time etc.

Conceptual analysis.

Thesis – antithesis – synthesis.

Elvaluative techniques for assessing children's work.

Value judgements.

Decision making.

(Batteries of tests evolved by a group designated as Educational Psychologists.

Child Centred Education (Piaget and all that!).

Free discipline (a contradiction?).

Group teaching.

Family grouping.

Vertical streaming (to stream or not to stream...)

Ability streaming.

Parental involvement and the eruption of Parent/Teacher

Associations.

The language concerning what and how and why teachers were teaching in the schools suddenly burgeoned with a whole new vocabulary designed to infuse the Scholastic system with new impetus and wider directions. Significantly, most of the authors of all these brave new 'concepts' had never been involved with the day-to-day teaching of young children but that is not to de-value the 'new' insights but for most teachers it was all too much and too fast for them to accommodate.

Knotty little topics such as:

How do you know that you know?
Is the school an institution of social change or does it merely reflect values and attitudes of the society it serves?
Training and Education.
Self-realisation.
Moral and Religious Education.
Indoctrination of children.

began to appear in Educational journals.

The confidence derived from the practice of tried and known procedures and routines was undermined by the bombardment of such radical and wide-sweeping challenges to the established order of their careers as teachers. There were breakdowns; there were resistances to any suggestion of change; there were exits into other more rewarding and less demanding forms of employment.

I knew that my enthusiasm to take responsibility for a village School, although valuable, was not enough. I had to know why and my assessor would want to know why! Although I met with his requirements there was always so much more to learn through those years of being in charge of a village school.

And there are always more problems which demand continued enquiry, reflection and dialogue between all those concerned with the education of successive generations. (And that means all of us!)

Suggestions for Discussion

"Small is beautiful." – Advantages/disadvantages (in human terms)
Teacher pupil/ratio. – factors to determine feasibility; possibility of helpers – students etc; 'statemented' children
For teachers, pupils, community – Public and private lives; School as a community as part of larger community – values and morals

Locality schools. – Rural areas; urban areas

The Teachers.
Experience – narrow and specific, with reference to national curriculum tests; wide within the system – personal interests (is it an either/or?) references to psychological definitions of introvert – extrovert personality

Further education? – In which areas? P.R. – public speaking; reading and reflection – writing – analysis of current trends; materials and publication; time to be made available!

Motives. – Personable ambition? Dictated by financial needs; lifestyle – a quiet life? (a fallacy!) Profession conviction
Who makes the appointments? Long term – short term

Church Schools.
Ownership and responsibility – morally and financial; historical background

Diversity of religious faiths.

Specialist small schools? Problems arising at secondary level...

C.F.N. Ireland
Education detached from religious teaching?
Introductory courses in Ethics and Civics; (rules and laws) moral values...

The System

Values and rewards! A good school (ups and downs!) A "good teacher...; payments by results, size of a school (again!)

Respite for teachers – part-time work for older teachers? Possibilities for experience in other kinds of schools – bridge building with the Independent schools; time made available for participation in politics! (non-party)

The Inspectorate and Advisors – their role as it is! and what it might be!!

Centralisation and role of L.E.A.s